OXFORD REVISION GUIDES

AS & A Level
COMPUTING
through diagrams

Ian Simons

OXFORD
UNIVERSITY PRESS

Great Clarendon Street, Oxford OX2 6DP

Oxford University Press is a department of the University of Oxford. It furthers the University's objective of excellence in research, scholarship, and education by publishing worldwide in

Oxford New York

Auckland Bangkok Buenos Aires Cape Town Chennai
Dar es Salaam Delhi Hong Kong Istanbul Karachi Kolkata
Kuala Lumpur Madrid Melbourne Mexico City Mumbai Nairobi
São Paulo Shanghai Taipei Tokyo Toronto

First published 2002

British Library Cataloguing in Publication Data

Data available

ISBN 0 19 913433 2

10 9 8 7 6 5 4 3 2 1

Typeset and designed by Fakenham Photosetting Ltd

Printed in Great Britain

Acknowledgements
The publishers would like to thank the following for permission to reproduce photographs: p5 The Office of the Data Protection Commissioner (both); p9 Science Photo Library/James King-Holmes; p17 Hewlett Packard (both); p19 Science Photo Library (bottom); p49 Rex Features.

Cover photo by FPG International.
Illustrations by Matt Buckley, Stefan Chabluk, David Mostyn.
Technical illustrations by Fakenham Photosetting Limited.

Contents

Legal implications

Data Protection Act 1984

This act, updated in 1998, was established due to the concern of the public over data stored on computer systems about them and its effects on their personal privacy. Data users are the individuals, companies or organisations who collect, use and control personal data.

The Act sets out a number of principles to which data users must adhere:

1 The data must be gathered and processed fairly and lawfully.
2 The data must be held for lawfully specified purposes.
3 The data must only be used for registered purposes and disclosed only to registered persons.
4 The data must be adequate and relevant to the purpose for which it is held.
5 The data must be accurate and where necessary, up to date.
6 The data must be held no longer than is necessary for the stated purposes.
7 The data must be protected by appropriate and proper security measures.

Data subjects are the people about whom data is collected. Under this Act they have the right of access to their personal data in order to have it corrected, updated or erased.

As a result of the Act, an office of Data Protection Registrar was established to ensure that all data users comply with the Data Protection principles.

Copyright, Designs and Patents Act 1988

Copyright relating to computing is infringed if a piece of software is copied, stored or modified without the permission of the owner. The software license purchased with the software usually outlines what can and cannot be done with the program. If a user does not have a licence, there is a fair chance that the software in the user's possession is illegal. Authors are therefore:

- Trying to make it more difficult for pirates to copy programs.
- Developing protection schemes for software.
- Trying to educate users about the rights of software distributors and the rights of buyers.

Computer Misuse Act 1990

Introduced primarily to prevent hacking and the spread of computer viruses, this act introduced three new offences relating to unauthorised computer access and to the unauthorised modification or deletion of data. They are:

- Unauthorised access to computer information.
- Unauthorised access with criminal intent.
- Unauthorised modification of computer information.

Hacking

This refers to someone attempting (being successful or otherwise) to gain unauthorised access to a computer system or particular programs or data stored on that system.

Virus

This is a program which can cause harm to a computer system. Viruses range from trivial to very serious and should be guarded against by installing antivirus software.

Types of software package

Word processing

This is probably the most common applications package used today. Its interactive nature enables the user to enter and edit a document, to print part or all of the document, and to store the work for future use.

User interface	Facilities	Communication	Uses
• It is similar to many other software packages, thus enabling the user to use pull down menus and short cuts etc • Help facilities available on line • The user is generally able to use this package to good effect fairly quickly even at a basic level	• Font or font size • Alignment • Spell and grammar checkers • Headers and footers • Tab setting • Columns and tables, add, delete, move and correct text • Use templates • Use mailmerge with a database • Colour and shading	• A word processing document can be attached to an e-mail for easy communication • It can be saved on a floppy and does not take up much space	• Write letters • Prepare worksheets • Business correspondence • Generate professional contracts, news reports etc

Spreadsheets

This applications package enables a user to enter data into cells which are presented in a table. The table consists of rows and columns which make the program most suitable for numerical tasks. The cells typically contain labels, values or formulae used with accounting, record keeping, statistical analysis, financial planning etc.

User interface	Facilities	Communication	Uses
• Includes the standard menu and pull-down options • Cut, paste and edit features are similar to other packages • Can prove quite difficult to manipulate the data especially with beginners and the non-mathematically minded • Help options available	• Enter values and text • Use formulae • Create graphs and charts • Insert, delete, copy and move rows and columns • Use in built maths functions • Format cells • Use macros • Query the spreadsheet	• Can be attached to an e-mail • Can be copied into a word processing package • Can be easily saved onto a floppy	• Banking and building societies, accountants, finance houses • Engineering, mathematical modelling • Teaching and training

Database

This type of package is used in many organisations to record data relating to its employees. A file structure is established and the data is entered, usually via a keyboard. Data can be added, updated, deleted and searched for with relative ease.

User interface	Facilities	Communication	Uses
• Includes many of the standard features such as menus and short cuts • Help option available • Can be difficult to set up if the tables are to be normalised, otherwise it is fairly straight forward with flat files	• Enter data into fields • Built in validation can be easily used • Diaries, forms, tables and reports used • Can be merged with a word processor package • Macros can be entered • Formulae can be used • Extensive query options	• Easily saved on disc • Files can become very large thus making communication slow • Reports can be copied into word processing documents	• Payroll, employee records • Stock item recording etc

Desktop publishing (DTP)

This is basically an extension of word processing and provides a user with greater control over all aspects of document design. It is usual to produce the text on a word processor (text editor), the graphics in an art package, and then create and manipulate the document using a desktop publishing (DTP) package.

User interface	Facilities	Communication	Uses
• Similar in many ways to a word processing package • Help options available • A wide range of special features used for design	• Import text and graphics • Text wrap around the graphics • Image control • Full use of colour • Enhanced page layout features • Tables and columns	• Documents can be large with embedded graphics, therefore data requirements needs more memory, hence slower transfer • Saved on to disc • Attached to e-mail • Stored as CD if very large	• News reports and magazines • Graphics and design

Computerisation implications

Employment v unemployment
Computerisation has had a major effect on jobs and the ways in which they are done. Jobs have been lost due to the introduction of robots and electronically controlled machines. Car manufacture was revolutionised during the 1980s, many jobs were lost but new jobs were created using IT. The steel, shipbuilding, newspaper and aircraft industries all went through a serious transformation and adopted an IT solution which helped to maintain their survival

New working practices using IT were essential for the majority of businesses to survive in a technology-driven world. Clerical work, banking, insurance, retail shopping, telecommunications, advertising, all embraced IT and made possible the necessary changes to working practices and environments.

Computer crime
With the introduction of electronic funds transfer (EFT), automatic teller machines (ATM), sensitive data and storage and computer controlled devices came the new generation of criminal. Despite the numerous safeguards put in place to protect data, unauthorised access and fraud still occur.

Health and safety
It was thought that the advent of computerisation would reduce people's working time, allowing them to enjoy more leisure. This has not happened and people seem to be working harder and longer instead. One outcome of this is the increase in health problems, particularly stress, repetitive strain injury (RSI) and eye strain.

These and other health and safety issues need to be given careful and serious consideration by employers if the workforce is to perform effectively.

Artificial intelligence and expert systems

Artificial intelligence (AI) refers to machines which mimic the way humans perform. Areas of study include chess, reasoning programs, natural language recognition and expert systems. As computers become more powerful and computer languages, such as Prolog, enable the computer to develop with rules and relationships, then AI will make some progress. At present, no computer has even the most basic human characteristics.

Expert systems
An expert system is a specialised computer program which has been created using a body of knowledge usually drawn from a number of human expert sources. The knowledge base can be added to or amended as and when new knowledge becomes available. For example, an expert system could be created with the aid of financial consultants in relation to savings plans, stocks and shares, investment and so on. This program could then be used to provide expert advice on a range of financial matters.

Expert systems (or knowledge-based systems, KBS) usually have the following features:

- Knowledge base – containing all the facts and rules concerning the topic of study.
- Interface engine – containing the software to create, manipulate and manage the body of knowledge and its interrelations.
- User interface – enabling the user to communicate effectively with the computer system, using the appropriate terminology and question styles.

Advantages	Disadvantages	Uses
• Many experts can contribute to and monitor the knowledge base • Always available • The KBS can be updated as and when required • May give answers/responses which are not mainstream	• Limited to a specific topic / area of knowledge • The advice is only as accurate or up to date as the knowledge in the system • Users can be over reliant on the machine	• Medical diagnosis • Financial advice • Construction • Government procedures • Law (acts and cases) • Geological surveys • Engineering

Design, manufacture and learning

Computer-aided design (CAD)

With the advent of very large storage systems and fast processors came the powerful CAD packages. This enables drawings to be created very quickly (compared with manually produced) and provides a number of special features which could be applied to drawings, such as swapping components around, repositioning parts in relation to others, zooming in/out, performing calculations, 3-D modelling and stress analysis, which is part of finite element analysis (FEA).

Advantages	Disadvantages	Uses
• Production of very accurate drawings • Create and manipulate objects with relative ease • 3-D modelling • Rotational views • Wide range of editing tools • Large component libraries • Easy to change/update drawings	• The packages are very sophisticated and take a long time to learn how to use • Require a lot of computer tmemory	• Engineering • Architecture • Design industry • Manufacturing

Computer-aided manufacture (CAM)

For many years much of the machinery used in the manufacturing industry was manually controlled by skilled operators. Although expert guidance is still required for use and safety, computers can be used to very good effect. The degree of accuracy can be increased and repetitive tasks can be computer controlled. Machines used in drilling, milling and lathe turning can all be operated under computer guidance.

Advantages	Disadvantages	Uses
• Machines can work consistently at a high degree of accuracy and repeatability • Computers can monitor speed, depth, size etc and produce reports • Can be used with CAD: CAD/CAM	• Safety features are much more strict as machinery is involved • Computers provide an added expense to the already expensive machinery	• Manufacture of components • Oil rigs • Geological explorations • Education and training • Mass production and rapid prototyping

Computer-aided learning (CAL)

This refers to the production of computer-based programs for people who wish to learn using a computer. Working within a full multimedia environment has made this a fun way to learn, where users work at their own pace and often in their own time. Much of the CAL material is available on the Internet or purchased on CD-ROM.

Advantages	Disadvantages	Uses
• Programs are available covering a wide range of study areas • The program can be re-run as and when required • The advanced technology makes the learning totally interactive, exciting and fun • Work at user's own pace	• The programs are limited to specific subject areas • Used extensively could hinder social skills • If the instructions or the material is not understood, there are limited alternatives to help	• Education • Training • Internet • Simulation

Computers in control

Computers can control all types of mechanical device. They can be used fairly simply to control the programs via a microprocessor in a washing machine, or to coordinate and control the complex circuitry in a sophisticated industrial robot. The principle of **feedback** is central to all computer-controlled applications, and this is achieved via sensors, analogue-to-digital converters, activators and transducers.

Advantages	Disadvantages	Uses
• Can work 24 hours per day • Consistent performance • Can do repetitive tasks with ease • Can be used in dangerous or hazardous conditions • Very accurate • Can be reprogrammed • Can be reused • No fatigue or health problems	• Can be very expensive • Limited in what they can do • Can cause many redundancies • Lack of human touch • Require high level of expertise to set up	• Car manufacturing • Steelworks • Chemical plants • Industrial Plants • In the home • Medicine • Security and safety

Computer simulation

Computers can be used to predict or simulate possible outcomes to given events. These computer-based models are only as accurate as the data, programs, hardware and assumptions on which they are built. Computer simulation refers to the development of a physical system to allow the users to study its behaviour under a variety of different situations and circumstances. Examples are:

Engineering simulations

These allow engineers to establish the strengths and weaknesses of possible designs: for example, bridges and buildings, without having to physically build the real thing. This saves time and money and enables possible redesign and experimentation to take place.

Medical simulations

These allow doctors to study the behaviour of organs or limbs in a variety of different scenarios. For example, operations can be simulated using life-like dummies.

Flight simulations

These enable trainee pilots to practise their skills in an artificial cockpit of the type of aircraft they are learning to fly. Using a computer to produce lifelike experience, the pilot can be assessed and monitored at each part of the flight.

Weather simulations

These enable meteorologists to predict the weather patterns that are most likely to occur, based on the current weather conditions. Very powerful computers are used to process the vast amount of data and to enable the weather team to make accurate predictions.

The Internet

The Internet is a huge network of networks which connects computers all over the world. It is commonly referred to as the 'net'.

The main communication links are provided by communication companies and governments, which are called NSPs (network service providers). These NSPs are collectively referred to as the Internet backbone. When we use the Internet, we are connected to the next level down, called ISPs (Internet service providers). It is via ISPs that we are connected to the backbone.

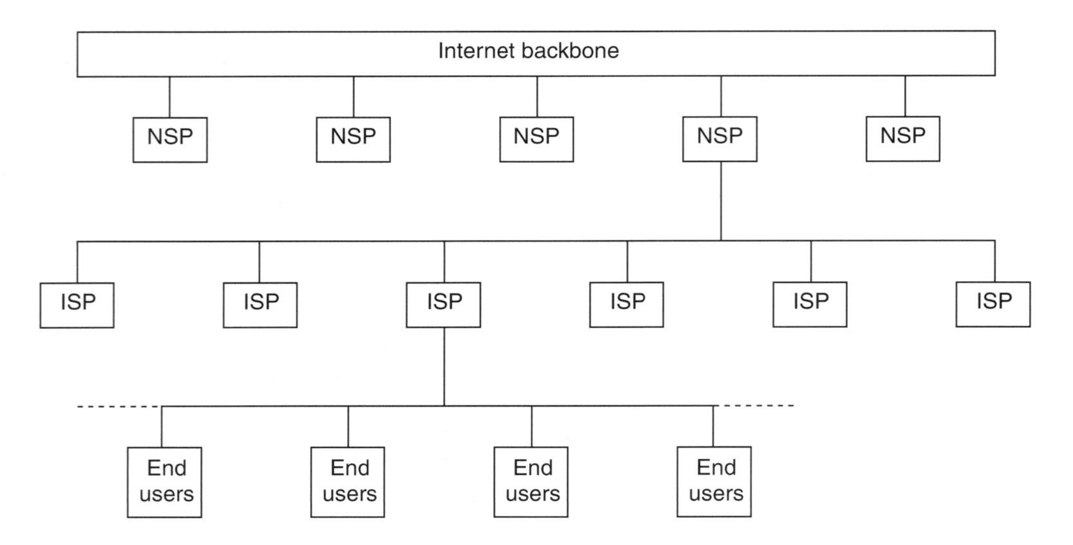

Computer users should be familiar with the following features of the Internet.

Videoconferencing
With video cameras attached to their computers users can communicate very effectively over great distances. For example, with the appropriate software in place, businessmen in London, Glasgow, Cardiff and Belfast could have a meeting with each other without actually leaving their offices – saving time, money and extensive travel.

E-mail
Electronic mail is now one of the main forms of communication between people and between businesses. For the price of a local call, a message can be sent anywhere in the world. The software that allows users to send e-mails also enables them to attach files containing pictures, text and graphs; keep an address book of notable e-mail addresses; forward messages to others; and send a message to a group of addresses at the same time.

Usenet
This enables users to get in contact with other users to discuss topics of interest. This could be used to good effect to enable people to share information or buy and sell products or just have fun. However, some of these user groups have promoted undesirable material.

Internet relay chat (IRC)
This enables users to actively engage in live conversations. People world wide who have the relevant IRC software can contribute to the debate on a particular issue. When on-line, everyone instantly has access to each other's messages.

E-commerce
The Internet is an ideal forum for buying and selling services and goods. On-line banking allows the account holders to pay bills, set up standing orders, transfer money, get statements and so on. People can also shop from the convenience of their own homes for a wide variety of goods. However, until consumers feel totally convinced that their credit card details will be completely safe when paying for goods in this way, it may take some time before this type of shopping fulfils its potential.

Internet search engines
The World Wide Web is enormous and still growing. Search engines were set up to help users to filter this mass of data and to help them get the information they are looking for. By typing in key words and refining searches, the search engines can locate the relevant sites. Common examples of search engines are: Yahoo (www.yahoo.com), Altavista (www.altavista.com), Google (www.google.com), Excite (www.excite.com).

The Internet (continued)

Web browsers
This is the software used to view and download web pages. The two main web browsers are Microsoft Internet Explorer and Netscape Navigator. By typing the web address or clicking on the 'hot link', the web browser program enables a user to view (browse) the site. Some features of a web browser are: keeps a history of pages visited within a time period, bookmarks pages, downloads files, browses forward and back through recent pages, links to search engines and accesses e-mail.

File transfer protocol (FTP)
This is a method used for transferring files across the Internet. One of its key features is uploading pages onto a website. Once a website has been created using Dreamweaver, Frontpage or some other program, the site, using FTP, can go live and the user's work is available to other users.

Uniform resource location (URL)
A URL basically represents address information and is commonly used to find documents on the net. To find a specific website, the URL could be typed in and the protocol http (hypertext transfer protocol) would be used to establish the connection, as shown below.

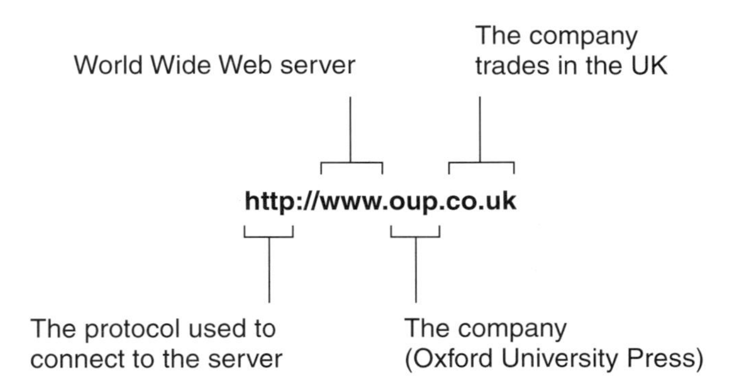

Every website has a unique IP (Internet protocol) address, which consists of four sets of three digit numbers separated by full stops, for example:

123.456.789.101

Because they are too difficult to remember, each home-page uses a domain name like the one above and this is mapped onto the IP address by the computer for ease of use.

Intranet
This is basically an in-house Internet. It is used by schools and other organisations to share documents, files and applications. The data can be filtered to keep out unwanted material and can be controlled centrally.

Intranets are usually based in local area networks (LAN) or are accessible only from within the organisations that host them.

Input

Devices connected to a central processing unit (CPU) are referred to as **peripherals**. Although these items are outside the CPU, they are connected via a range of input ports and associated driver software to the CPU and are under its control. They can be used to customise a computer to individual needs.

A simplified computer system is shown below.

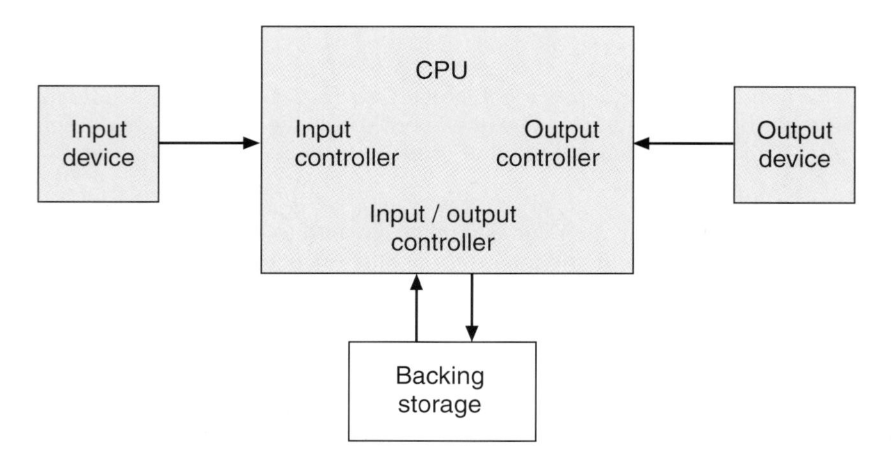

Keyboard
This has been the main input device for many years and will probably continue to be so for the foreseeable future. Most keyboards have a QWERTY layout (the letter keys along the top row) and are well suited for typing in commands, entering data into a document or filling in data on a predefined form / template.

Advantages	Disadvantages	Cost	Speed
• Commonly used • Standard layout of keys • Inexpensive	• Easy to make typing errors • Constant use can lead to RSI • Need to learn to type if high input speeds are to be achieved	• £10 – £25 for basic models • £50+ for more specialist keyboards	• Depends on the operator

Mouse
Due to the popularity of the **graphical user interface** (GUI), the mouse has become a standard feature on almost all computer systems. When the ball in the bottom of the mouse is moved, it generates a signal which corresponds to the movement in an (x, y) direction. A mouse can have one, two or three buttons and even a wheel to enable scrolling in a document. The most common is two buttons. The left button is used to select and the right button is used to give a menu.

Advantages	Disadvantages	Cost	Speed
• The (x, y) movement on the desk corresponds to the (x, y) pointer movement on the screen. • Point and click • Inexpensive • Ideal for selecting and drawing	• Unclean environments can cause problems for mouse ball movement • Easily broken or stolen • Need for hand–eye coordination	• A few pounds for the cheapest • £40+ for infrared or specialist mouse	• Depends on operator and conditions

Light pen
This device reads light from a display screen, thus allowing the user to point to specific areas and modify or change them.

Input (continued)

Advantages	Disadvantages	Cost	Speed
• Users can see where they are drawing • Fairly easy to use • Can be used for drawing or writing • Can reduce need for keyboard use	• Not very precise • Needs specialist software • Becoming less popular • Quite expensive • Can be tiring on the arm	• Several hundred pounds • Can depend on the software options	• Depends on the operation: handwriting, drawing – slow; selecting – fast

Touch screen

This is a special kind of screen that is sensitive to touch. Infrared beams cross the screen vertically and horizontally thus enabling the software to detect the position where a touch took place. The selection is recorded and the necessary action is carried out.

Advantages	Disadvantages	Cost	Speed
• Very easy to use • Ideal for non-computer users • Well suited to shopping centres, banks and libraries • Can eliminate use of keyboard	• Specialist software is often needed • Limited in operations that can be done • More expensive than standard VDUs	• Several hundred pounds plus, depending on size of screen	• Depends on the operator's ability to interpret what the program offers

Joystick

Joysticks are mainly used for games, virtual reality walk-throughs and controlling robots. The device is either held in the hand or stands on a desk. The main handle has several buttons on it, usually used for firing missiles or hand-to-hand combat. Additional buttons can be placed around the device to give a variety of special features which are specific to the application.

Advantages	Disadvantages	Cost	Speed
• Enables simulation • Provides a full range of movement • Great fun to use • With practice very good control can be achieved • Ideal for games	• Can be difficult to control movement • Limited use • Cheaper models are easily broken or damaged	• £10 – £20 for basic models • £80+ for more robust and sophisticated models	• Practice makes perfect

Key to disc

This input method is generally used with applications using large batches of data. The input is keyed in at a keyboard and copied onto a magnetic disc or tape. Data can be validated by the program as it is being entered and then verified later when another operator keys it in for comparison. Any discrepancies are recorded and corrected before being stored on the disc. Many large organisations provide a multi-station system in order to generate the vast amount of data needed for processing.

Advantages	Disadvantages	Cost	Speed
• Data is prepared off-line thus ensuring it is as complete as possible when used for for processing • The on-line process is very efficient	• Costly in terms of human and computer resources • Faster and more efficient methods are available: for example, OCR technology • Dedicated hardware and specialist software are needed	• Very expensive	• Determined by the speed of the operator, the number of operators and the quantity of data needed to be processed

Input (continued)

Optical mark recognition (OMR)

Optical mark recognition (mark sensing) is mainly used with multiple-choice type documents for market research and multiple-choice tests. The responses to the questions are given by shading one of the options, then the document is read and marked automatically by the computer. The reader records the response by noting the position where a mark was made. Marks are determined by evaluating the light reflecting off a page; a pencil mark will reduce the reflected light thus establishing a mark. An example of OMR use is the National Lottery (Lotto) form.

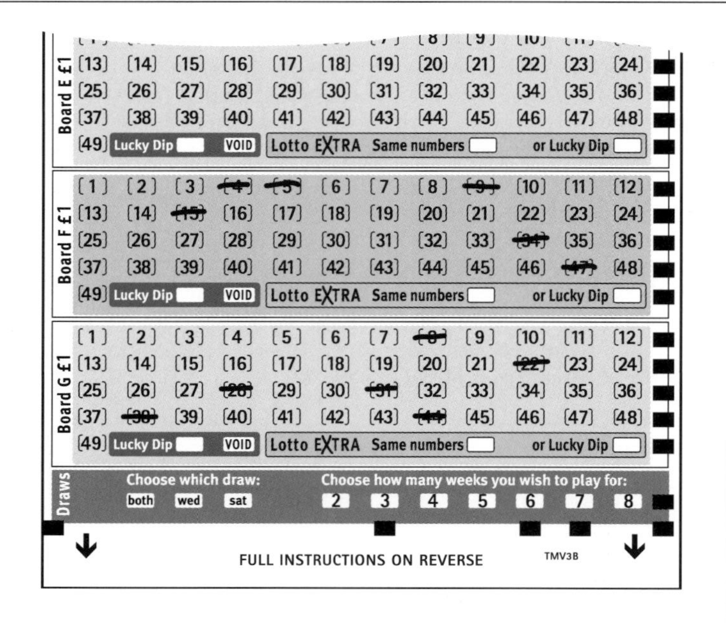

Board E £1
[13] [14] [15] [16] [17] [18] [19] [20] [21] [22] [23] [24]
[25] [26] [27] [28] [29] [30] [31] [32] [33] [34] [35] [36]
[37] [38] [39] [40] [41] [42] [43] [44] [45] [46] [47] [48]
[49] Lucky Dip VOID Lotto EXTRA Same numbers or Lucky Dip

Board F £1
[1] [2] [3] [4] [5] [6] [7] [8] [9] [10] [11] [12]
[13] [14] [15] [16] [17] [18] [19] [20] [21] [22] [23] [24]
[25] [26] [27] [28] [29] [30] [31] [32] [33] [34] [35] [36]
[37] [38] [39] [40] [41] [42] [43] [44] [45] [46] [47] [48]
[49] Lucky Dip VOID Lotto EXTRA Same numbers or Lucky Dip

Board G £1
[1] [2] [3] [4] [5] [6] [7] [8] [9] [10] [11] [12]
[13] [14] [15] [16] [17] [18] [19] [20] [21] [22] [23] [24]
[25] [26] [27] [28] [29] [30] [31] [32] [33] [34] [35] [36]
[37] [38] [39] [40] [41] [42] [43] [44] [45] [46] [47] [48]
[49] Lucky Dip VOID Lotto EXTRA Same numbers or Lucky Dip

Draws
Choose which draw: both wed sat
Choose how many weeks you wish to play for: 2 3 4 5 6 7 8

FULL INSTRUCTIONS ON REVERSE
TMV3B

Advantages	Disadvantages	Cost	Speed
• Low error rate • Very fast reading of many documents • Statistical reports easily generated • Ideal for data capture requiring large quantities • Can be read manually	• Rejected documents have to be marked by hand. • Only suitable when high volume, limited response data is needed • Marks must be accurately and clearly recorded or they will be misread • Limited number of possible responses	• Small machines can cost a few hundred pounds. • High-speed, powerful machines cost many thousands of pounds	• High speed which varies proportionally with cost

Optical character readers (OCR) and scanners

Optical character readers are more sophisticated than mark sense readers in that they can recognise letters, numbers and special characters rather than just marks. The same process of reflected light is used but with OCR each character produces a pattern that is compared and matched with a set of stored patterns.

Scanners with OCR software can scan in a page incorporating text and enable the user to edit the text. This saves much time by eliminating rekeying, particularly when there is a substantial amount of text to edit.

Advantages	Disadvantages	Cost	Speed
• Documents do not have to be retyped or redrawn • The sophisticated software means greater flexibility with handwriting • The scanning process is quite fast and generally very accurate	• The original document has to be clean and handled with care • The hardware and software can become very expensive • Poor quality documents could be rejected • Misread documents have to be re-entered	• Basic devices can be around £100 • The faster, more precise, high-quality machines can cost thousands of pounds	• Depends on the resolution needed • Depends on price and paper size

Input (continued)

Magnetic ink character readers (MICR)

Magnetic ink character readers are used mainly in banking for processing cheques. The ink contains iron oxide particles which are magnetisable and therefore easily and quickly read by a special reading head. The characters along the bottom of the cheque represent the cheque number, branch sort code, and account number. After the cheque has been cashed, a magnetic ink encoder is used to print the amount of the cheque along the bottom line. The cheque is now ready for processing and usually clears within three or four days.

Although this system is used extensively by banks, it is old technology and could soon be replaced with the latest OCR systems.

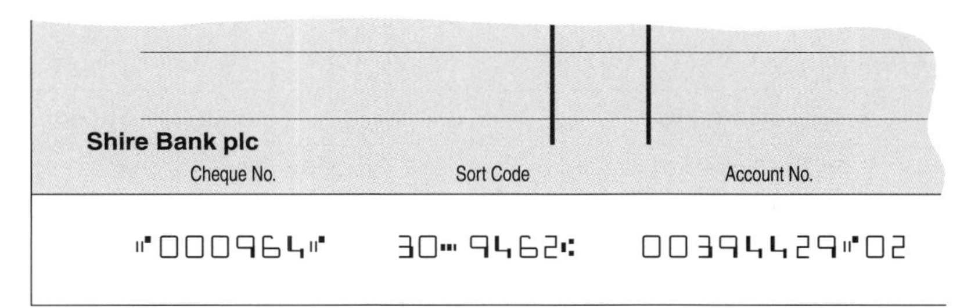

Advantages	Disadvantages	Cost	Speed
• The ink can be read by humans and machines • It provides high degree of security • Very difficult to forge • Thousands of cheques can be read in minutes • Cheques can be read even if creased or dirty • Very reliable	• Very high quality printing is needed to produce the cheques • The hardware and associated software is very expensive • Limited in the applications and operations it is used for	• Very expensive since it is specialised equipment	• Extremely fast – thousands of cheques can be read each minute

Barcode readers

Barcodes are used to identify goods sold in supermarkets and shops. A barcode consists of a pattern of wide and narrow stripes which encode a number. The EAN (European Article Number) is used to code most products in the UK. The bar codes are read by an optical wand, a bar code scanner or a bar code reader.

Note The EAN Association prevents repetition and ensures the validity of barcodes.

Advantages	Disadvantages	Cost	Speed
• Very fast and accurate method of data capture • Barcodes can be read in any direction • A barcode uniquely represents one product type • Easy to use by checkout attendants • Use of check digits ensures validity of data	• Relatively expensive to install • If the barcode is misread, it either has to be scanned again or manually entered at the checkout.	• The hardware and software are still expensive but the price has greatly reduced over the years	• Depends on operator

Input (continued)

Electronic funds transfer (EFT), magnetic stripes, smart cards

Most banks offer electronic funds transfer in the form of **automatic teller machines** (ATM). A plastic card is used by the customer to perform the financial transactions. The card has the account number and the credit limit encoded on it. A PIN (Personal Identification Number) is entered along with the card for added security.

Plastic cards are used in a variety of applications: for example, phone cards, bus and rail tickets, theme park passes. The magnetic stripe is used to encode up to 220 characters and cannot be read by humans.

A smart card has a microchip embedded in it, which is capable of storing large amounts of data and even being updated when required. Because of the chip, a smart card is almost impossible to copy and can provide the user potentially with a greater range of options and information.

Advantages	Disadvantages	Cost	Speed
• Easy to use • Convenient • Cards can be easily disposed of when out of use • EFT saves the user from carrying cash • Smart cards are very secure	• Easily stolen or lost • Some people do not feel comfortable with this technology • The magnetic-stripe cards can be copied easily	• The cards are free provided the user meets the provision criteria • The invisible cost is added to the services	• Generally fast and convenient

Voice

Technology is now available, albeit limited, whereby a user can talk into a microphone and his/her computer would respond either by showing the words on the screen or acting on commands.

Advantages	Disadvantages	Cost	Speed
• A user can dictate a message and print it or save it for future use • Ideal for disabled people • Suitable for hands-free applications	• The system may not recognise the user's voice • Prone to errors at present unless the system is trained to recognise the user's voice • Inflexible with relation to multi-users	• Limited systems cost about £50 • Advanced versions cost hundreds of pounds	• Depends on the operator and the recognition ability of the system

Sound

Many devices exist to enable users to create, record, store and control sounds. Musical Instrument Digital Interface (MIDI) is used extensively by musicians to enable them to put keyboard, guitar or voice into a computer so that it can be manipulated to their desired end. Special software can translate what is played into a musical score, which can be transposed or changed in other ways.

Advantages	Disadvantages	Cost	Speed
• Once the data is in the computer, it can be arranged in many different ways • A single musician can use overlays to create a whole band sound • Musical scores are easy to produce	• The recording equipment can be expensive • A single user would need to know how to play a musical instrument before being able to take full advantage of this technology	• MIDI equipped keyboards are a few hundred pounds • The sky is the limit. It depends on what is needed and wanted	• MIDI is recorded instantaneously

Output

Viewing the output from a computer system can be achieved in a number of different ways and for a number of different reasons. In this section, only the main output peripheral devices will be considered.

Printers

A wide range of printers were once common. However, this selection, in terms of popularity, has narrowed down considerably, and two printers dominate the market: the **ink jet printer**, which represents the main device for educational, home and small business use, and the **laser printer**, which is extremely popular in all aspects of computing.

Ink jet printer

These printers are excellent for personal use and provide a high-quality printout, especially on good, graded paper. The characters are formed by spraying ink through very fine jets on to the page. Its most appealing features are the use of colour and the quality pictures that it can produce. Ink jet printers are still much slower than laser printers but provide excellent value for money and meet most people's printing needs.

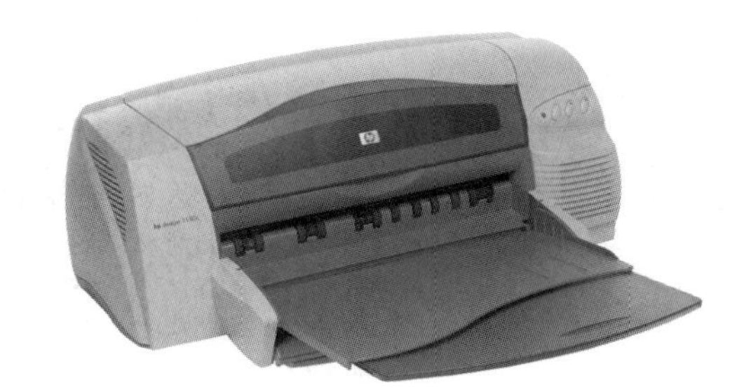

Advantages	Disadvantages	Cost	Speed
• Inexpensive • Very good quality printouts • Colour • Quiet • High-quality paper gives excellent printouts • Driver can be downloaded via the Internet	• Relatively slow compared with laser printers • Can be expensive for A3 models • Ink cartridges are expensive	• Can range from £50 to several hundred • Ink cartridges are expensive, £20–£30 each	• 4–8 pages per minute

Laser printer

The laser printer is probably the most complete printer available. Its one main drawback is price, although this recently has reduced greatly. Mono-laser printers can be purchased for a few hundred pounds but the colour versions are still very expensive for personal and small business use. A laser printer uses toner which is attracted to a drum when it is charged electronically and rotated.

Advantages	Disadvantages	Cost	Speed
• Excellent quality printouts • High speed • Quiet • Colour is available • Very reliable • Fairly inexpensive to run	• Colour versions are expensive • Need to be maintained, which could be expensive	• Mono from a few hundred pounds • Colour from a few thousand pounds	• Range 8–24 pages per minute

Output (continued)

Computer output on microfilm (COM)

Computer output on microfilm (and microfiche) is a process of photographically producing documents and reducing them in size so that many of them can be stored in a small space. Microfilm refers to a roll of 16 mm film, whereas microfiche relates to a sheet of film which can store 100–300 documents per sheet.

COM is particularly suited to applications where large volumes of data need to be archived, such as in libraries. Using a special reader to magnify the document, the user can access the data in a read-only setting.

Advantages	Disadvantages	Cost	Speed
• Large volumes of data can be stored in a very small area • Readers are inexpensive	• The data is read only • Finding specific documents might prove time consuming especially on the manual systems • The data is not easily updated. For example, if data is incorrect, a new sheet of film needs to be produced	• Readers are a few hundred pounds • Machines to produce COM are thousands of pounds	• Depends on the operator and the type of reader used

Plotters

These are used to produce high-quality drawings. Straight lines, curves and text can be printed with tremendous accuracy, thus creating detailed and complex drawings with relative ease. There are two main types of plotter: the **flatbed** and the **drum**. On the flatbed plotter, the paper is placed on the bed (or table) and an arm containing one or more pens moves forwards in two directions (*x* and *y*), backwards or along the bed. The pens can be a variety of different colours and thicknesses and are computer controlled to produce the drawing.

On the drum plotter, the arm is fixed, and the paper can be moved backwards and forwards over a drum or rollers. The computer controls the movement of the paper. These plotters can produce large technical drawings at high speed.

Another use for plotters is the cutting of vinyl film for making large signs and banners which are used extensively in advertising.

Advantages	Disadvantages	Cost	Speed
• High-quality, accurate drawings • Various thicknesses and colours of pens • Large-scale drawings possible • Drawings can be fully annotated	• Large, specialist plotters can be very expensive • Only a few pens can be used at a time	• £50–70 for the basic models • Several thousand pounds for the very large, specialist plotters	• Depends on the cost and the size and complexity of the drawing

Visual display unit (VDU)

The computer monitor has become the standard item of output equipment for the vast majority of users. They have become more sophisticated over the years and are generally priced in accordance with their key features: size, colour and resolution.

- The size of the screen is measured diagonally with 15 in being fairly typical. However, now the price of the 17 in monitor has been much reduced, it is becoming more popular, particularly as most of an A4 page can be viewed on the screen with minimal scrolling.
- The resolution refers to the number of **pixels** (picture elements) used to represent a full screen. VGA (video graphics array) are 640 × 480 pixels. SVGA (super VGA) are 800 × 600 pixels. This is fairly standard on most home-use systems. XGA (extended GA) can give up to 1600 × 1600 pixels. However, digital provides 6 000 000 × 6 000 000 pixels. It is important to realise that the graphics card inside the computer has to be suitable to support the resolution type. A rough guide is:
  SVGA → 8–16 Mb graphics card
  XGA → 16–32 Mb graphics card
  Digital → 64–128 Mb graphics card
- If one bit is used for each pixel, then $2^1=2$ colours are available. If 8 bits are used then $2^8=256$ colours are available. Using 16 bits gives $2^{16}=65\,536$ colours per pixel. It is clear that the high number of available colours combined with the high resolution requires a graphics card with enough memory to support it.

Storage

The main memory of any computer system is limited in terms of its size, speed and volatility. In order to store data for future use, some form of secondary storage is required. In this section, a selection of storage peripheral devices will be considered.

Floppy disc

This is a 3.5 in magnetic disc which has become a standard feature on most microcomputer systems. Typically, it can store 1.44 Mbytes of data but with advanced compression techniques a floppy disc can store in excess of ten times that amount. The floppy consists of a thin plastic disc encased in a rigid protective plastic cover. A metal sliding shutter moves aside when the disc is placed into a drive, enabling the read / write heads to access the disc surface. It is possible to protect the data from being accidentally overwritten by sliding a write protect tab in the bottom corner of the disc.

Before data is stored on a disc, it has to be formatted. This involves the creation of a magnetic map in terms of tracks and sectors which enables data to be written to and read from the disc directly.

Zip disc

This disc requires its own drive and can store much more data than the standard floppy. Typically, a zip disc can hold 100 Mbytes, but a recent version holds 250 Mbytes. A super floppy is available which allows standard floppies to be used in the same drive. It can hold 100 Mbytes.

Hard disc

It is now fairly standard for a PC to have a hard disc capacity of 10–80 Gbytes. The disc is housed in a sealed unit, which keeps out dirt and dust particles. It rotates at a very high speed and the read / write heads hover just above the surface. The hard disc is an aluminium platter coated with a magnetic material. It is divided into hundreds of concentric tracks and a number of sectors. Each sector contains between 256 and 512 bytes, and this represents the smallest unit of data transfer.

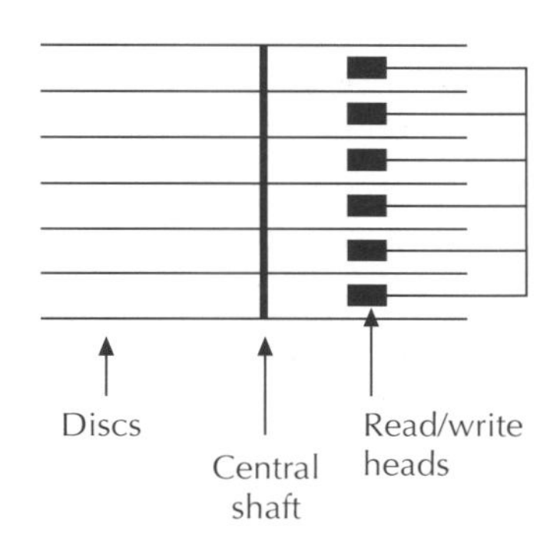

As well as the fixed hard disc unit, there is also an exchangeable disc pack unit. This is where a number of platters are connected to a central shaft. The read / write heads for each surface are mounted on one unit where they all move in and out together to read from or write to the various tracks. As the read/write heads move between the tracks, a cylinder of information is created.

Compact disc read-only memory (CD ROM)

This is rapidly becoming a standard feature on most PCs, especially with the recordable options available. Because of its high capacity (650 Mbytes), high speed and low cost, it could replace the floppy drive. The CD is made from a polycarbonate material coated with aluminium. At manufacture, a powerful laser burns pits into the surface of the disc at specific locations. Where a pit has not been burned, the surface area is called 'land'. Unlike the hard disc, the CD contains one single spiral track and it is made up of lands and pits. These lands and pits represent the binary digits needed to store pictures, sound, text etc.

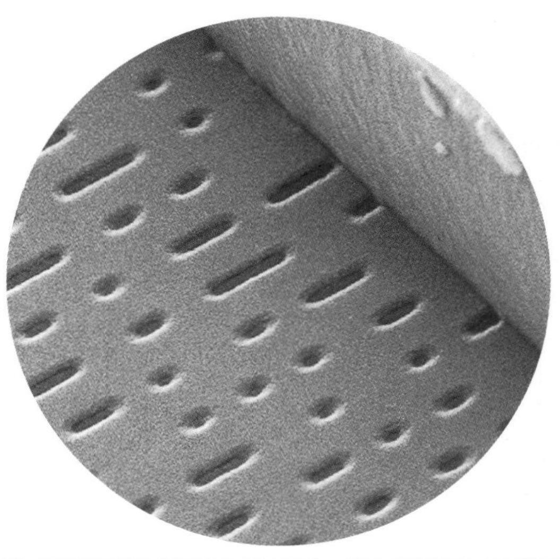

Storage (continued)

Digital versatile disc (DVD)
This technology was originally intended for video recordings and games. It has an extremely high capacity (up to 20 Gbytes) and could in time replace the CD ROM. Some PCs are providing a dual CD/DVD drive to allow for both technologies side by side.

Write once read many (WORM)
These are sometimes referred to as CD Gold because the colour of the disc is gold. These are CDs which, when written to, cannot be altered and therefore require some preparation for the content. They are ideal for archived data and are available for home use as well as the larger, faster, higher capacity specialist use. The common WORM drive on many modern PCs is the CD-R drive.

Magnetic tape
Tape is still an ideal medium for back-up because it is fast, inexpensive and has a high storage capacity. Data can only be read from or written to the tape when it is moving at full speed over the read / write head. For this reason, data is usually stored in blocks (a group of records treated as one unit) with an interblock gap to allow for slowing down and speeding up between 'reads' and 'writes'.

The number of records in each block is referred to as the **packing density**.

The tape is made of plastic with a magnetisable material attached. Data is stored in tracks (usually nine) which run the full length of the tape. The data is recorded in frames across the tape so that one byte and a parity bit are represented on each frame.

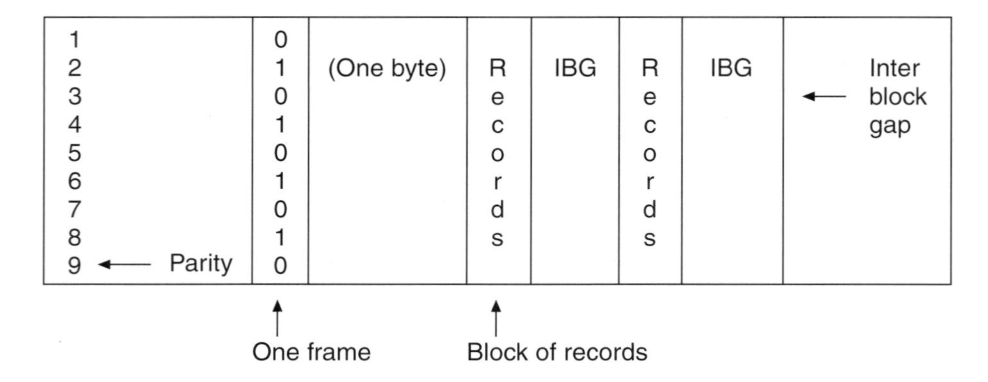

Tape streamers
These machines can use very small cartridges at high speed and with high capacity. They are ideal for back-up with the small business market. The larger tape streamers are mainly used for batch processing on minicomputers and, more especially, mainframe computers.

Digital audio tape (DAT)
The DAT cassette is small but unlike conventional tape it has the tracks running across the tape instead of along it. This means that the read/write heads have to move quickly in order to produce the high speeds. DAT can store over 20 Gbytes on one cassette, making it extremely popular for mass back-up, especially with pictures and sound.

DAT is often used for backing up smaller PC-based networks.

Computer bit patterns

Our everyday counting system is in (base 10) (denary), which is why the following place values are used:

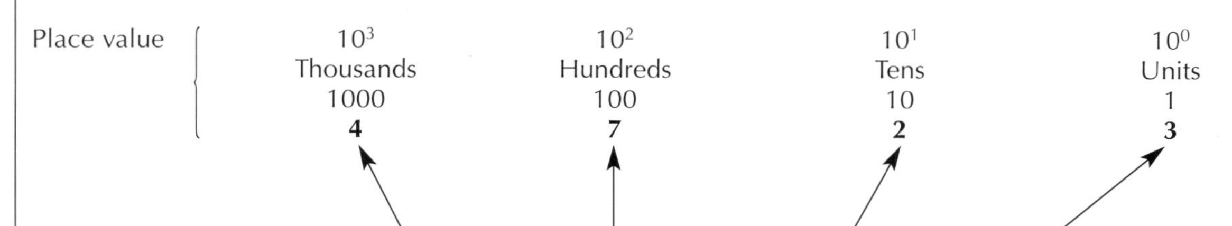

In the example, there are 4 groups of 1000 + 7 groups of 100 + 2 groups of 10 + 3 units.

Note Any number raised to the power of zero equals 1.

However, as shown below: digital devices work in base 2: that is, **binary**. They therefore use different place values.

1 bit gives two options: 0 or 1. This is ideal for electrical switches, which have two states: ON or OFF

$2^0 = 1$
$2^1 = 2$
$2^2 = 4$
$2^3 = 8$
$2^4 = 16$
$2^5 = 32$
$2^6 = 64$
$2^7 = 128$

8 bits = 1 byte. This can provide 256 different binary arrangements from 00000000 to 11111111: that is 0 to 255

Note The first counting number is 0 not 1. Therefore, 8 bits are 0, 1, 2, 3, 4, 5, 6, 7.

Key terms

Bit Binary digit: 0,1.

Byte 8 bits, which can represent a single character.

Word One or more bytes which can be addressed and processed as a single unit.

An example of the application of the binary system is given below.

Place value	2^7	2^6	2^5	2^4	2^3	2^2	2^1	2^0
	128	64	32	16	8	4	2	1
Binary number	1	1	1	0	0	1	1	1 = 231

That is, one group of 128, one group of 64, one group of 32, one group of 4, one group of 2 and one unit represents the number 231 (base 10).

Coding systems

Digital computers make extensive use of the binary system to represent data such as letters, numbers, pictures and sounds. The characters which a computer can process form the character set of that particular computer. There are two main methods of coding used by computers.

ASCII – American Standard Code for Information Interchange. This uses a 7-bit code with an extra bit added for checking purposes. It is very popular with PCs.

EBCDIC – Extended Binary Coded Decimal Interchange Code, pronounced 'eb-see-dic'. Used by large computer systems.

There are other coding systems in existence and they are suited to specific areas of computing: for example, UNICODE.

UNICODE This is a 16-bit coding system which can represent 2^{16} (65 536) different codes.

UNICODE is already supported in Java, a high-level language, and it is likely that, because of the extensive range of options for storing and transporting data and codes, UNICODE will be more widely used in future. There is a UNICODE consortium which sets this standard and if international standardisation takes place, UNICODE may well displace ASCII and EBCDIC.

A sample of ASCII codes and their decimal values

Character set	Decimal equivalent	Binary code						
A	65	1	0	0	0	0	0	1
B	66	1	0	0	0	0	1	0
C	67	1	0	0	0	0	1	1
D	68	1	0	0	0	1	0	0
E	69	1	0	0	0	1	0	1
F	70	1	0	0	0	1	1	0
G	71	1	0	0	0	1	1	1
H	72	1	0	0	1	0	0	0
I	73	1	0	0	1	0	0	1
J	74	1	0	0	1	0	1	0
K	75	1	0	0	1	0	1	1
L	76	1	0	0	1	1	0	0
M	77	1	0	0	1	1	0	1
N	78	1	0	0	1	1	1	0
O	79	1	0	0	1	1	1	1
P	80	1	0	1	0	0	0	0
Q	81	1	0	1	0	0	0	1
R	82	1	0	1	0	0	1	0
S	83	1	0	1	0	0	1	1
T	84	1	0	1	0	1	0	0
U	85	1	0	1	0	1	0	1
V	86	1	0	1	0	1	1	0
W	87	1	0	1	0	1	1	1
X	88	1	0	1	1	0	0	0
Y	89	1	0	1	1	0	0	1
Z	90	1	0	1	1	0	1	0
Space	32	0	1	0	0	0	0	0
0	48	0	1	1	0	0	0	0
1	49	0	1	1	0	0	0	1
2	50	0	1	1	0	0	1	0
3	51	0	1	1	0	0	1	1
4	52	0	1	1	0	1	0	0
5	53	0	1	1	0	1	0	1
6	54	0	1	1	0	1	1	0
7	55	0	1	1	0	1	1	1
8	56	0	1	1	1	0	0	0
9	57	0	1	1	1	0	0	1
+	43	0	1	0	1	0	1	1
–	45	0	1	0	1	1	0	1
=	61	0	1	1	1	1	0	1
?	63	0	1	1	1	1	1	1
.	46	0	1	0	1	1	1	0
;	59	0	1	1	1	0	1	1

Character set The set of symbols that may be represented by a computer and typically include: letters, spaces, numbers, punctuation marks and control characters.

Each character is represented by a unique ASCII value.

Binary, octal and hexadecimal systems

Denary	Base 10	Has 10 digits, 0–9.
Binary	Base 2	Has 2 digits, 0 and 1.
Octal	Base 8	Has 8 digits, 0–7.
Hexadecimal	Base 16	Has 16 values, 0–9 plus A=10, B=11, C=12, D=13, E =14 and F=15.

Conversion from denary to binary

By putting appropriate binary values above the binary code and adding the values together where 1 is represented.

```
        32  16  8  4  2  1
23 =         1  0  1  1  1   = 16 + 4 + 2 + 1 = 23
```

By continually dividing by 2 and recording the remainder. Answer: 10111.

```
2 |23
2 |11  R1
2 | 5  R1
2 | 2  R1   ↑
2 | 1  R0   |
    0  R1   |
```

Conversion from denary to octal

By putting appropriate octal values above the octal code and adding the values together where a number is represented.

```
      64  8  1
67 =   1  0  3 = 64 + 3 = 67
```

By continually dividing by 8 and recording the remainder. Answer: 103.

```
8 |67
8 | 8  R3   ↑
8 | 1  R0   |
    0  R1   |
```

Conversion from denary to hexadecimal

By putting appropriate hexadecimal values above the hexadecimal code and adding the values together where a number is represented.

```
       256  16  1
108 =    0   6  C = (6 * 16) + 12 = 108
```

By continually dividing by 16 and recording the remainder. Answer: 6C.

```
16 |108
16 |  6  R12  ↑
      0  R6   |
```

Fractional numbers in binary

Place value: 32 16 8 4 2 1 . $\frac{1}{2}$ $\frac{1}{4}$ $\frac{1}{8}$ $\frac{1}{16}$

So $9\frac{1}{2}$ gives: 1 0 0 1 . 1

- 1 → One group of eight
- 1 → One unit
- 1 → One half

which is: $8 + 1 + \frac{1}{2} = 9\frac{1}{2}$

Binary coded decimal (BCD)

BCD

Each decimal (denary) digit is represented by four binary digits. For example, 427 in denary gives:

Base 10	4	2	7
Place value	8 4 2 1	8 4 2 1	8 4 2 1
Binary value	0 1 0 0	0 0 1 0	0 1 1 1

So, 427 in BCD is 0100 0010 0111.

Advantages	Disadvantages
• Easy to calculate • Accurate representation of numbers	• Takes up a lot of space • Only deals with positive values • Calculations can be difficult

Range of values in BCD

0 = 0000	2 = 0010	4 = 0100	6 = 0110
1 = 0001	3 = 0011	5 = 0101	7 = 0111
	8 = 1000	9 = 1001	

Images, sounds and signals

Sound

Sound can be captured using a microphone, CD or tape, or using a musical instrument with MIDI (Musical Instrument Digital Interface). Sound waves are continuous (analogue) and therefore need to be converted into a digital format if the data is to be used by a computer. An **analogue-to-digital converter** is used to change the analogue sound waves into a digital binary pattern.

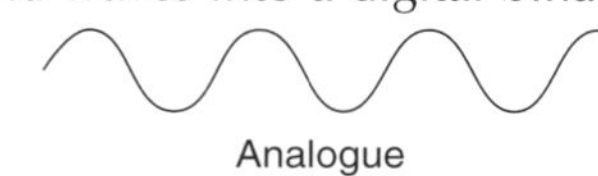

Digital

Bitmap graphics

Each dot (or **pixel**) on the screen is represented in a file. When colour is used, more bits need to be stored. Bitmap images use the same number of pixels no matter what size the image becomes. Therefore, enlarged images may appear grainy. Bitmap images are also called **raster images**.

Vector graphics

With vector graphics, lines are stored as equations and represented in vector format. Each line has its attributes stored and therefore are easy to change without loss of resolution. When a vector graphic image is enlarged, the whole image increases while maintaining the resolution.

Key terms

Pixel Picture element: that is, each dot on the screen.

Resolution The number of pixels used to represent an image.

High resolution This is where millions of pixels are used to represent an image. It provides excellent quality but uses a lot of memory.

Low resolution Generally associated with pictures which are represented by large blocks of colour: for example, TELETEXT images.

Monochrome A screen with two states – each pixel is either on or off. This means it is a 2-bit image.

Colour depth The number of colours in an image varies. These are stored as different numbers of bits depending upon the number of colours required. Each pixel requires a number of bits. For example, 8 bits gives 256 colours, 16 bits give 65 536 colours but uses a lot of memory. One bit stores two colours

Graphics card This is a piece of hardware fitted inside the computer and used to store the information needed to represent images on a screen

Converters Two types: analogue-to-digital (ADC) and digital-to-analogue converter (DAC)

Lossy and lossless compression Some file types retain their data no matter how many times they are transferred, while others loose resolution each time they are copied or transferred. For example, GIF files are lossless compression files (no data is lost): 8 bit colour is used, giving 256 colours. JPEG files are lossy compression files (data is lost): 24 bit colour is used, giving 16 million colours.

Data and information

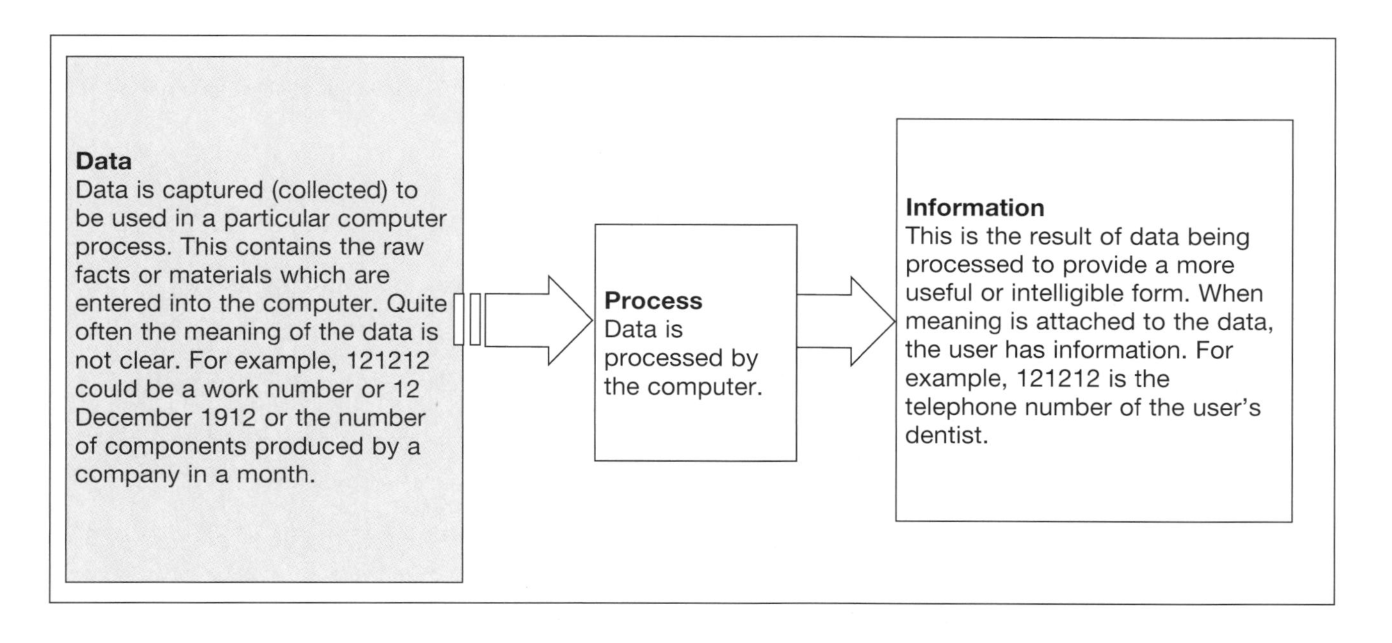

Data sources

Direct
When data is gathered and used for a specific purpose, this is direct use. For example, the names and addresses of people who want newspapers delivered to their homes. Their requests are met and newspapers are delivered on the days they request. Then money is collected each week or month.

Newspaper delivery √

Indirect
When data is used for a different purpose from that for which it was gathered, this is indirect use. For example, the list of people wanting newspapers delivered receive information about home insurance. The original data is used for a completely different reason.

Newspaper delivery ×
Home insurance √

Some data types

Integers	Such data represents the full range of whole numbers, both positive and negative.
Real	Such data represents all numbers which include a fraction or a decimal point.
Pure binary	Such data represents numbers using base 2. For example: 2^6 2^5 2^4 2^3 2^2 2^1 2^0 64s 32s 16s 8s 4s 2s 1s 1 0 0 1 1 0 0 one group of 64 + one group of 8 + one group of 4 In base 10, this gives 64 + 8 + 4 = 76. So, 76 (base 10) = 1001100 (base 2).
Boolean	Sometimes called logical data, it can only have one of two values – TRUE or FALSE, represented by 1 and 0.

Mathematical notations

Two's complement

This is a method of representing positive and negative numbers. The bits have the same place value as binary, except that the most significant bit (the leftmost bit) represents a *negative* value.

Place value	−64	32	16	8	4	2	1
Binary number	1	0	0	1	0	1	1

This gives −64 + 8 + 2 + 1 = −53

Maximum value = 63 ($2^6 - 1$); minimum value = −64 (-2^6).

The process of converting from a positive number to a negative in two's complement form is as follows. Using the binary form of the number:

1 Change the ones to zeros and vice versa. This is called one's complement.
2 Add one to get the two's complement. Note: the two's complement of a number is its negative representation.

So, for 18 we get:	−32	16	8	4	2	1	
	0	1	0	0	1	0	= 18
	1	0	1	1	0	1	One's complement
						+1	Add 1
Result:	1	0	1	1	1	0	= −18

Subtraction using two's complement

Take, for example, 26 − 19. Proceed as follows.

		−32	16	8	4	2	1	
Write binary pattern for 19:		0	1	0	0	1	1	=19
Change 0s to 1s and reverse:		1	0	1	1	0	0	One's complement
Add 1 to give –19:							+1	Add 1
		1	0	1	1	0	1	= −19
Write binary pattern for 26:		0	1	1	0	1	0	= 26
Add –19 to 26:	**1**	0	0	0	1	1	1	= 7

Answer is 7.

When there is an overflow bit, show it as such and state: 'Ignore it.'

Sign and magnitude

The leftmost bit in the pattern is the sign of the number

When the sign bit is 1, the number is *negative*. When it is 0, the number is *positive*. The remainder of the bits after the sign bit represent the size of the number in binary.

For example:

	16	8	4	2	1	
(1)	0	1	1	0	1	= **−13**

	16	8	4	2	1	
(0)	1	0	1	1	1	= **+23**

The sign bit has been circled in both cases.

Fixed point

Let's consider a 10 bit register

- If we require integer values only, then using two's complement notation we have the following range:

−512	256	128	64	32	16	8	4	2	1
*	*	*	*	*	*	*	*	*	*

  Maximum positive number is 0111111111 which equals 511
  Maximum negative number is 1000000000 which equals −512

- When we introduce a decimal point, the trade off is between the range of integer values and the range of fractional values. For example:

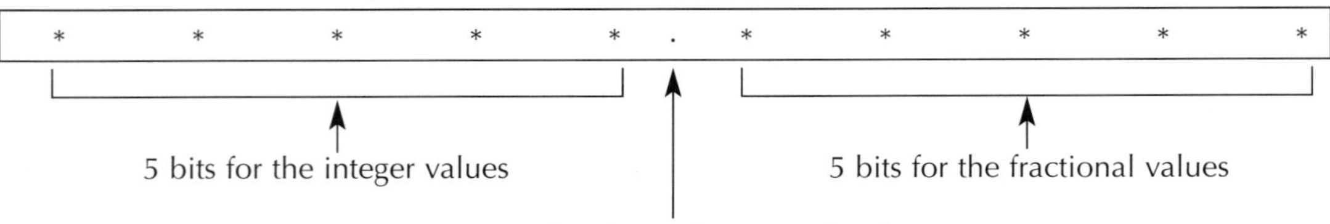

Note – The decimal point is fixed.

Mathematical notations (continued)

Floating point

This is a method of representing fractional values (or real numbers) and is similar to standard form. Floating-point notation increases the range of values which can be represented. The mantissa gives the accuracy and the exponent gives the range.

	6-bit mantissa		4-bit exponent			Represents 3 in binary. Therefore, move the digits three places to the left.
	0.10110		0011			
Values:	4	2	1	.	$\frac{1}{2}$	
Result:	1	0	1	.	1	

This gives $4 + 1 + \frac{1}{2} = 5\frac{1}{2}$

Normalization

This is a procedure that ensures the following:

- The most efficient representation of the number is achieved.
- Each floating point number can only have one representation.
- Maximum precision is achieved.
- Calculations are performed more accurately.

The examples will use a 6-bit two's complement mantissa and a 4-bit two's complement exponent.

Rules

1 For positive numbers, the mantissa must always start '0.1'. So: we place the first 1 in the binary code after the decimal point.

	−4	2	1	.	$\frac{1}{2}$
For the value $3\frac{1}{2}$:	0	1	1	.	1

Write 0.111 and use the exponent of 2 (10 in binary) to move the digits back.

Answer: 0.11100 0010 = $3\frac{1}{2}$

2 For negative numbers, the mantissa must always start '1.0'. This usually means stripping away leading 1s in the binary value.

	−4	2	1	.	$\frac{1}{2}$
For the value $-3\frac{1}{2}$:	1	0	0	.	1

Get the two's complement of $3\frac{1}{2}$:

−4	2	1	.	$\frac{1}{2}$	
0	1	1	.	1	= $3\frac{1}{2}$
1	0	0	.	0	= One's complement
				1	Add 1
1	0	0	.	1	$= -4 + \frac{1}{2} = -3\frac{1}{2}$

Notice it starts 1.0.

Mantissa is 1.001 and exponent needs to be 2 (10 in binary) to move the digits two places to the left.

Answer: 1.00100 0010 = $-3\frac{1}{2}$

Key terms

Overflow This term is used when the number is too large for the register which contains it.

Underflow This occurs when the number is too small for the register which contains it.

Truncation This involves terminating a number after a set number of significant figures or decimal places. For example:

1.236 truncated to three significant figures gives 1.23
3.456 truncated to one decimal place gives 3.4

Rounding This involves approximating a number to a set number of significant figures or decimal places. For example:

23.456 rounded to four significant figures gives 23.46
1.256 rounded to two decimal places gives 1.26

All computers need **software** (programs) to make them operate. The two main types of software are:

- **Systems software** These programs control and coordinate the hardware.
- **Application software** These programs enable the user to perform specific tasks, such as word processing, databases and spreadsheets.

The role of the operating system is to enable the user to concentrate on the task. Therefore, the complexities of working the hardware are largely hidden from view.

Types of operating system

Batch	• All the data to be input is gathered together and prepared off line using backup media until processing takes place. • Once the batch of data is complete, it is processed as a unit. • This method of processing is generally used with multiprogramming where several jobs are loaded together and processed. By switching between the jobs as and when required, the processor is used much more effectively.
Multiprogramming	• Two or more jobs/programs are held in the main memory by a process called **partitioning**. • Priorities may be given to jobs to facilitate processing. • The impression is given that the jobs are processed simultaneously but in fact they are processed in bursts controlled by the operating system. • Since the processor works at high speed compared with the peripheral devices, several jobs can benefit from processing time. While one job is waiting for an input, output or peripheral transfer, the other can receive the attention of the processor.
Interactive	• There is a direct communication link between the user and the system. • There is an immediate response from the processor: for example, getting information at an ATM or booking a flight.
Single user	• Only one user at a time can operate the computer in an interactive mode. • Only one user program at a time can be loaded into the main memory.
Multi-access	• Several users can communicate with the computer at apparently the same time via a terminal. • The processor gives a time slice to each terminal and, during that time allocation, processing that is needed is carried out. By rotating around the terminals on the system and processing in short bursts, each user has the impression that they are the sole users of the system.
Multitasking	• Multiple applications are able to be run at the same time by the processor.
Real time	• This is where the computer responds immediately to input data. It processes it and returns the output data. With such a speedy response, the output data can then be used to effect the next operation. Examples include air traffic control, chemical plants and missile defence. • This type of system is very expensive because of the nature of its applications.
Time sharing	• By swapping processes in and out of the main memory, the operating system can share the time given to each one.
Network	• This is used when a number of computers need to communicate with each other. • All the computers on the network must have the same operating system software to be able to communicate. • If a server is used, additional software is required. • The operating system can monitor and control user activity.
Multiprocessing	• This is where more than one processor is made available so that the processing requirements can be spread around.

Functions of an operating system

User interface
The operating system enables the user to make full use of the resources by coordinating the control of system software. The graphical user interface (GUI) has greatly helped to simplify the operational use of the computer.

Memory management
This requires the organisation of user programs so that they are stored and retrieved from memory as efficiently as possible. In situations where a program is too large for the immediate access store, a technique called **virtual memory** can be used. By splitting the program into blocks and swapping them in and out of the main memory, the program can be run giving the impression that there is more memory available than is actually the case.

Interrupt handling
The operating system has to handle a wide variety of interrupts and in many cases generate a response to inform the user of what is happening. Typical interrupts are: hardware device not working properly; waiting for a mouse click or keyboard response; no signal; drive fault; system error.

Resource management
Priorities and scheduling are important features which help to ensure that the most efficient use is made of the resources. Jobs can be given priority over others and a schedule of tasks can be established to fully utilise the hardware and processing capabilities. In certain situations, the same device may be requested from different jobs and it is the role of the operating system to manage these requests.

Security
The operating system controls all access to the hardware and software resources. A log of all operations can be created and a record kept of user activity. Taking back-ups of files can be done periodically under the supervision of the operating system.

Note These functions are not the only ones that the operating system performs but they provide an overview of the type of duties that so often are taken for granted.

File management

Everything stored on a disc is in a file. Each file has its own name and stores only one type of information. There are two main types of file: a **program file**, which stores a program (set of instructions), and a **data file**, which could be text, or pictures or sounds.

It is the responsibility of the **file manager** to enable the user to save, delete, copy, load, name and rename files. The arrangements surrounding the logical view of the files and the physical arrangement of the data on the disc are controlled by the file manager.

The file manager:

- manages disc memory allocation
- maps logical file addresses to physical file addresses
- manages directory, subdirectory and files.

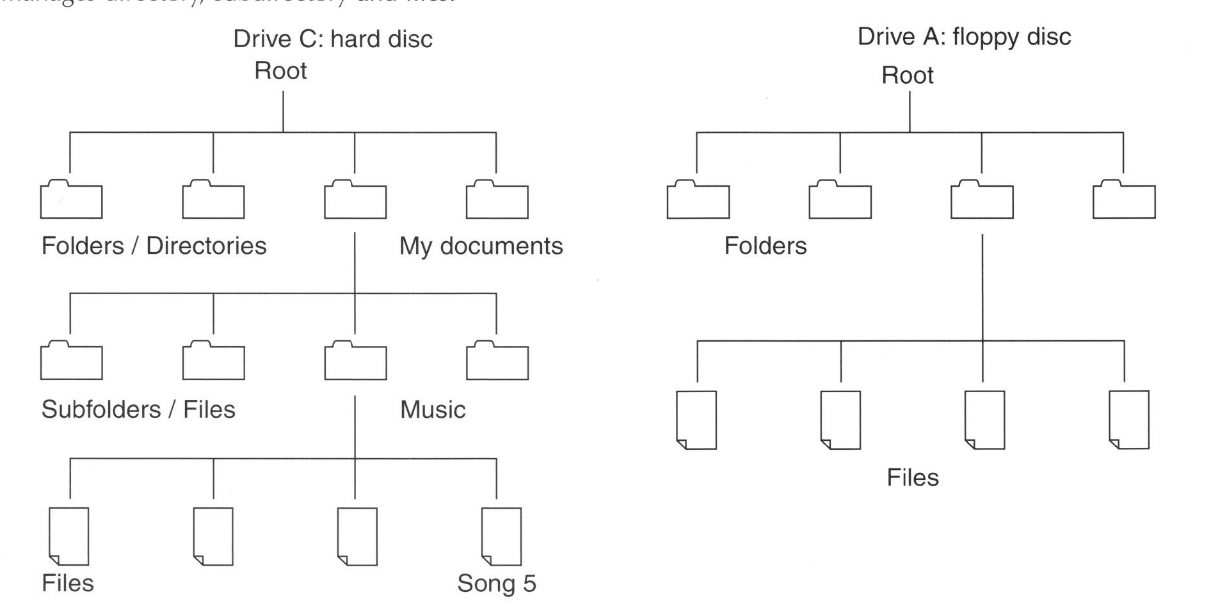

File management (continued)

A **directory** is a group of files and/or subdirectories. A **subdirectory** is a directory within a directory. (A directory is sometimes called a **folder**.)

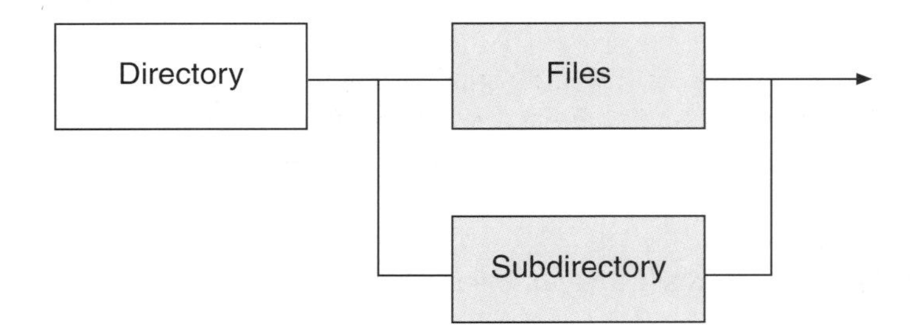

File

This can be information such as text (for example, a Word document (doc)), a picture (Tiff) music (MP3) or bitmap (bmp). Sometimes an extension is put onto the file name to help describe the file type: for example, doc, jgp.

Pathname

This is the path that needs to be followed from the root (start of the path) to the actual file. For example, to get Song 5 on the drive C use:

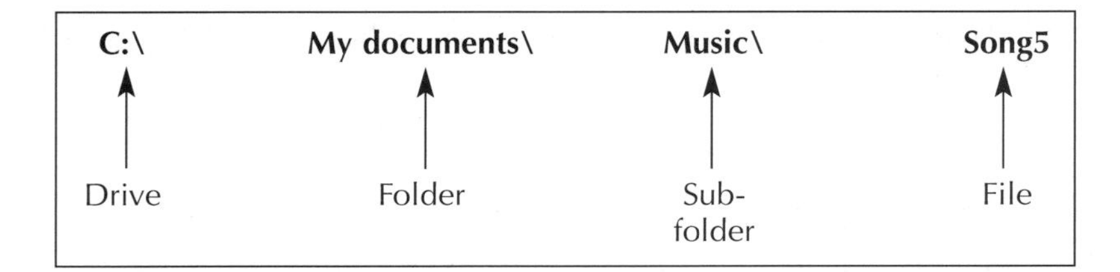

Blocks and buffers

Data is transferred to and from disc in blocks of, for example, 1k. This is the physical unit of transfer. A buffer is used to hold the data temporarily as it passes in and out of memory. Each block in memory is uniquely addressable, thus creating a very efficient and accurate means for management.

Access rights

This refers to the control provided for each directory, subdirectory or file. There are a number of different rights that can be given to users, such as:

- Read only
- Read/Write
- Certain directories only
- Erase permission
- Full control

Operating systems such as Windows 95 could only manage hard disc memory in approximately 1.7 Gb segments. Due to the increase in disc storage capacity, the computer operating system had to separate larger hard drives and pretend it had several hard drives. For example, a hard disc of size 6.3Gb would be divided into four logical drives, C, D, E, F.

Backing-up

This is a process of making sure that data is preserved for future use by taking copies of the files or folders. There are three methods which can be used:

- To take a back-up of all the files.
- To take a back-up of selected files.
- To take a back-up of changes since the last back-up.

It is sensible practice to take back-ups at regular intervals.

Archive

This is a copy of files and or folders which will be used for reference if required: for example, for auditing.

Input/output management

The input/output (I/O) manager is responsible for controlling and coordinating the flow of information to and from the I/O devices. The control signals for each device are unique and therefore require an I/O controller to link them with the processor. Each device has a program called a **driver** to allow and enable communication between it and the CPU.

Due to the nature of I/O devices, a series of interrupt signals are generated. An interrupt handler program is activated to deal with the processor, therefore buffers are used to store the data temporarily.

Memory management

The memory manager is mainly responsible for the main physical storage of the system and the processing that surrounds that vital resource. It is the role of the memory manager to convert the logical addresses used in the main memory.

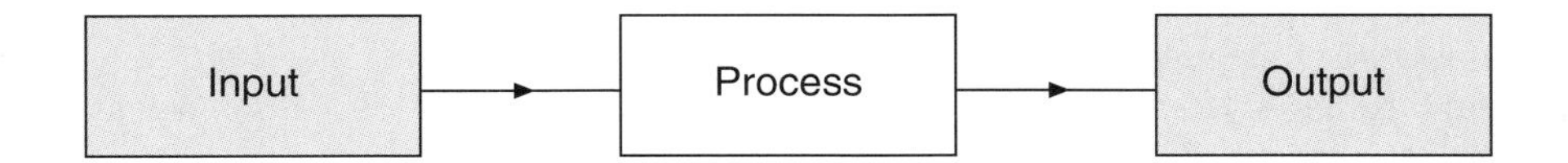

Each process that is carried out by the control unit has to be loaded into memory by a program called a **loader**. There are several types of loader programs:

- **Bootstrap loader** This is a program that loads itself by using call instructions to activate the whole program sequence.
- **Linking loader** This can be used to link several programs together and run them as one.
- **Absolute loader** This loads the program from an absolute memory location: that is, a specific area in the memory. As hardware and software are upgraded (as it inevitably will be), great problems can be caused for programs stored in this way.
- **Relocating loader** This can load the program anywhere in the memory thus enabling the operating system to make best use of the memory. Code can be stored in two ways:
  - **Absolute code** This refers to the static nature of the code once it has been placed in the memory.
  - **Relocatable code** This is code that can be moved to other memory locations easily.

Virtual memory
This is used when the amount of main memory required is not available.

The program is split into a number of conveniently sized segments and the blocks of data are swapped in and out of the main memory. The impression is that the computer has more memory than it actually has.

Paging
In paging, the immediate access store (IAS) is organised into a number of fixed units called **pages**. The logical pages can be stored in any physical memory page space

Pages can be stored on disc and swapped in and out as and when required

Dynamic linked libraries (DLL)
This refers to a collection of executable files that are activated by another program. When the main program is loaded into the main memory and executed, these library files are only used when needed and then replaced back into the library thus saving space and enabling a more efficient use of the processor. An example would be the print function used on all software packages.

Process management

The **process manager** is mainly responsible for the execution of programs and the variety of phases which they can undergo.

Process states

A process may be in one of three states:

- **Running** The process is using the processor.
- **Runnable** The process is ready to run but is waiting for the processor to become available.
- **Unrunnable** The process requires I/O and could not run even if the processor were free.

If running is suspended at any time, it may be necessary to save details of the exact point in execution when the interrupt occurred so that the process can resume from the exact same position.

Scheduling

Deciding which job is to be processed in a multiprogramming situation is the duty of the **scheduler**. Priorities can be set by the user or the operating system to help place jobs in order ready for processing. Setting priorities is a complex issue and the following factors have to be considered:

- Priority level given.
- How much CPU time is required.
- Peripheral transfers needed.
- How long the job has been waiting.
- What mode of operating system operation is needed.
- What resources are available.
- Avoiding deadlock.
- Job deadlines.

Note A program called the **dispatcher** is used to pass jobs to the processor.

In a batch situation, there are two main types of scheduling:

- **Job scheduling** The status of each job is established by considering the factors given above.
- **Process scheduling** This program works out what processor time and what resources are needed. The dispatcher then delivers the job that fits in with the **processing strategy** used in the selection process.

In a multi-access situation, process time can be allocated to each user in a 'round robin' fashion. The scheduling algorithm may determine a fixed time slice for each user in turn.

Deadlock is a situation when two processes require the use of a resource that the other is currently using and neither seems capable or willing to give up what they have.

Human–computer interaction (HCI)

This refers to the communication links between the user and the computer. A variety of approaches are used, as detailed below.

Command driven

The computer responds to a command or set of commands. These instructions enable the user to quickly instruct the computer. However, in order to use this approach the user must have a knowledge of the commands that are available and how they are used. For this reason, this approach is more suited to experienced users. An example is MS DOS, where the user responds to a system prompt: for example, >.

Menu driven

The user is presented with a number of options and a means of selecting them. There is no need to remember commands or rules. This approach is suited to beginners or novice users.

Graphical user interface (GUI)

This is certainly the most popular method used today. The user is presented with a set of options, often in icon (diagrammatic) format. The mouse pointer is used and a selection is achieved by clicking the mouse. Directories, files, devices and packages can all be represented by icons. This makes working the computer easier for novice users.

Once the user becomes more familiar and experienced with this environment, a set of short cuts can be used to help speed up operations.

Job control interface

This is suitable if a set of jobs or programs can be run under the direct supervision of the computer without any user interference. A specialised language is used (**job control language**) to control the running of the jobs in the computer.

This interface is ideally suited to payroll applications, where the programs run automatically.

Central processing unit (CPU)

In this section, the examples given relate to a fictional machine, because the actual architecture and instruction sets vary depending on the machine. The basic concepts are, however, transferable.

The machine architecture of the **central processing unit** (**CPU**) will now be considered, showing how its various components relate and work together.

The CPU is the brain of a computer and consists of three main parts: the **control unit**, the **arithmetic and logic unit** (**ALU**) and the **main memory**. However, the processor usually refers to a combination of the control unit, ALU and associated registers.

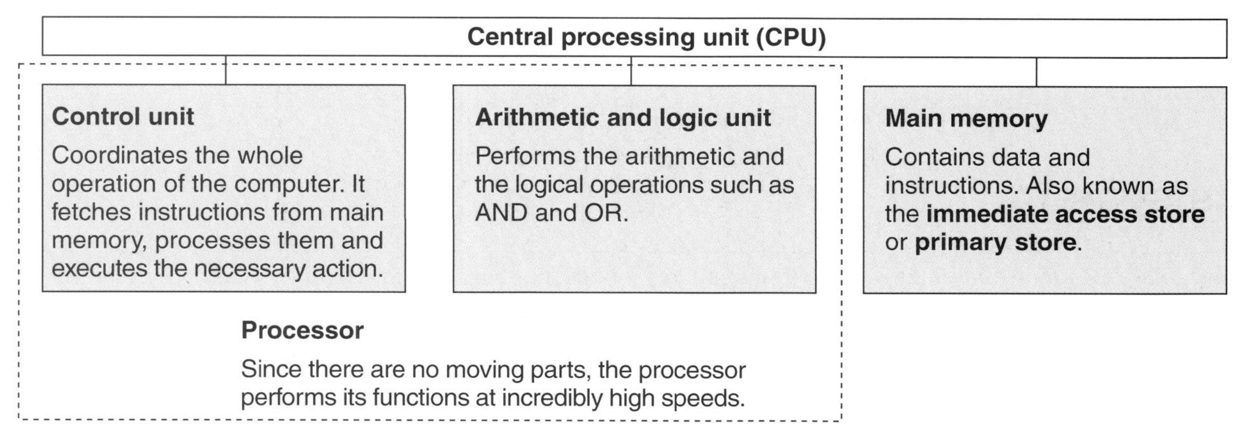

The functions of the processor are:

- To control and coordinate the operations for the whole system.
- To manage the main memory.
- To fetch, decode and execute instructions.

Because the processor is an electronic unit, it requires some method of synchronisation for its functions. This is carried out by the **system clock**, which triggers a pulse to keep the components in sequence with each other. The higher the clock speed, the faster the machine is able to function. For example, a 2 GHz processor performs 2×10^9 pulses per second.

The processor is connected via buses and lines to other parts of the system, and is supported in its operation by a selection of registers and I/O controllers.

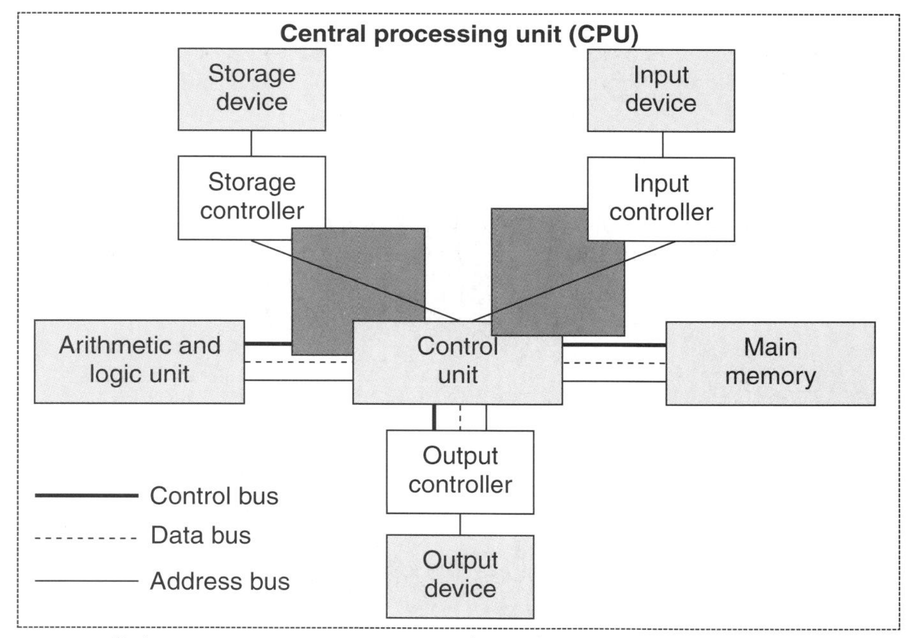

Inside a microcomputer, all the components are connected together using a system of **buses**. All peripherals, such as **input**, **storage** and **output** devices, have to be connected to this bus system. A piece of hardware called an **interface board** plugs into special sockets, which in turn are connected to the bus system.

Immediate access store (IAS)

This has a large set of uniquely addressable memory locations in which to store data and instructions. Because the computer stores everything in binary, there is no distinction between the data and instructions and this is determined only by the context with which it is used.

Central processing unit (continued)

Interface
This is the hardware and associated software required for communication between a peripheral device and a processor.

The interface compensates for the difference in operation between the components.

Input/output controllers
These items of hardware enable a number of peripheral devices to be connected to the processor. Some controllers are specific to the peripheral device, while others are more versatile and can be used by many devices.

Some controllers are input only, output only or both.

Bus system

Buses are the communication links which connect the various components of a computer. Three buses are used in this high-speed system. They are **address**, **data** and **control** buses.

Address bus
This bus carries identification about where data is being sent. Addresses can only travel in *one* direction along the bus.

The number of address lines determines the amount of addressable memory cells. For example, 16 lines gives $2^{16} = 65\,536$ addressable memory cells.

Data bus
This bus carries the actual information, either data or instructions. Data signals can travel in *both* directions along the data bus.

The number of data lines determines the processing capabilities of the processor and its ability to process the instructions word size.

Control bus
This bus carries control signals about the data and addresses being sent around the computer system. They can include information about when data is to be transferred, the type of data and the operations to be performed.

Control signals can travel in *both* directions along the control bus.

Registers

A register is a special purpose temporary storage location. Although registers are similar in structure to the locations in the main memory, they can be accessed and altered much more quickly. There are five main types of register:

Current instruction register (**CIR**) Instructions from memory are placed in the CIR so that the contents can be decoded and executed. Also called an **instruction register**.

Sequence control register (**SCR**) This register holds the address of the next instruction (or piece of data) to be fetched from memory. Also called a **program counter**.

Memory address register (**MAR**) This register is used to locate the address of instructions or data in the main memory.

Memory data register (**MDR**) All instructions and data pass in and out of main memory via MDR. Also called a **buffer register**.

Accumulator This is a special register associated with the ALU, which can carry out basic arithmetic operations, such as addition and subtraction. Most computers have many accumulators within the processor.

Other registers

Process status register (**PSR**) This is a hotch-potch of unrelated flag bits used by the processor to keep track of the program as it is being fetched and executed. This would be different for different processors.

Z	N	P	1	V	C	I	B
Set to zero	Negative result	Positive result	Always one	Overflow	Carry bit is used	Interrupt	Break

Stack pointer This register is used to select the top value on a data structure called the **stack**. Data is pushed onto the stack and popped off it. This is called a **lifo** (last in first out) data structure because the last item in will be the first item out.

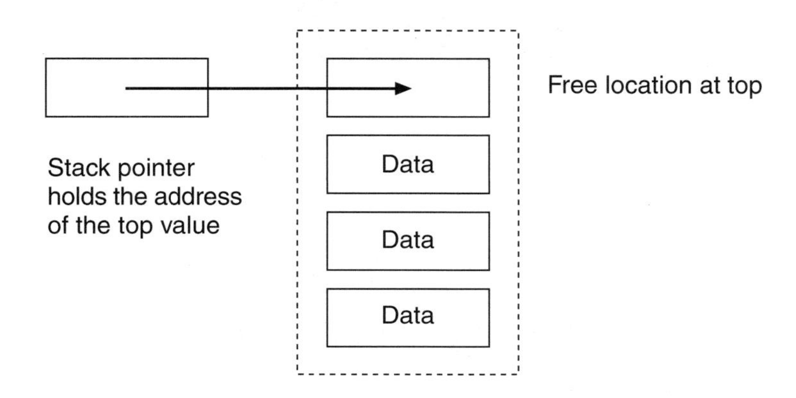

Fetch–decode–execute cycle

The control unit is the part of the CPU which manages the execution of instructions. Each instruction is fetched in sequence from memory, decoded and executed by sending the necessary control signals to the various parts of the computer. This cycle, shown below, can be repeated millions of times per second.

Fetch phase

Step 1 Load the memory address register (MAR) with the address of the next instruction to be executed.
Step 2 The data is retrieved from memory via the memory data register (MDR).
Step 3 The data is placed into the current instruction register (CIR).

Movement (decode) phase

Step 4 The sequence control register (SCR) is incremented by 1 so that the processor is ready to start the cycle from the next location in sequence.

Execute phase

Step 5 The data in the CIR is decoded.
Step 6 The instruction is executed.

Arithmetic and logical operations

Arithmetic operations

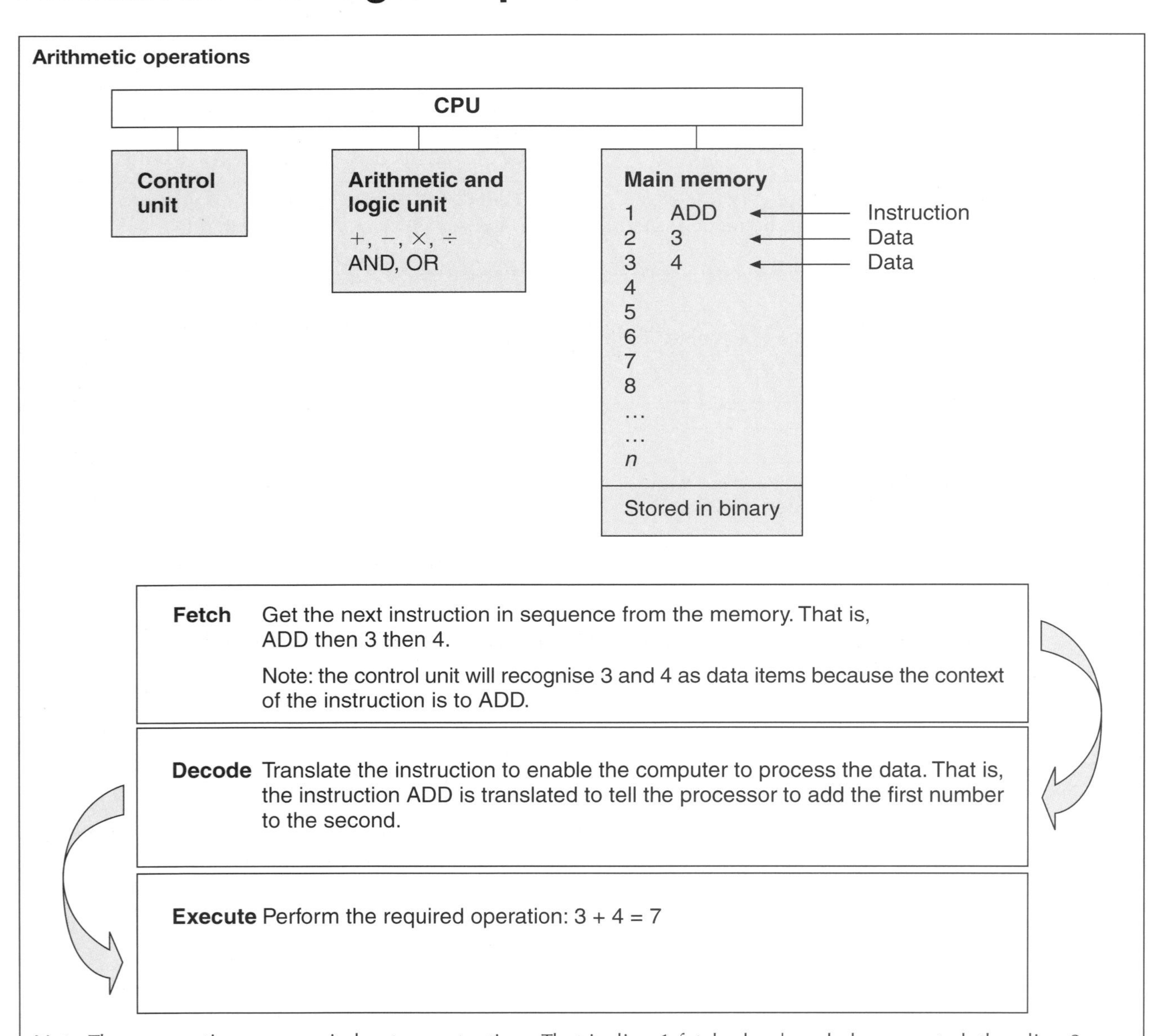

Note These operations are carried out one at a time. That is, line 1 fetched – decoded – executed, then line 2, then line 3.

Arithmetic and logical operations (continued)

Logical operations

Here is the program to determine the date of the Battle of Hastings.

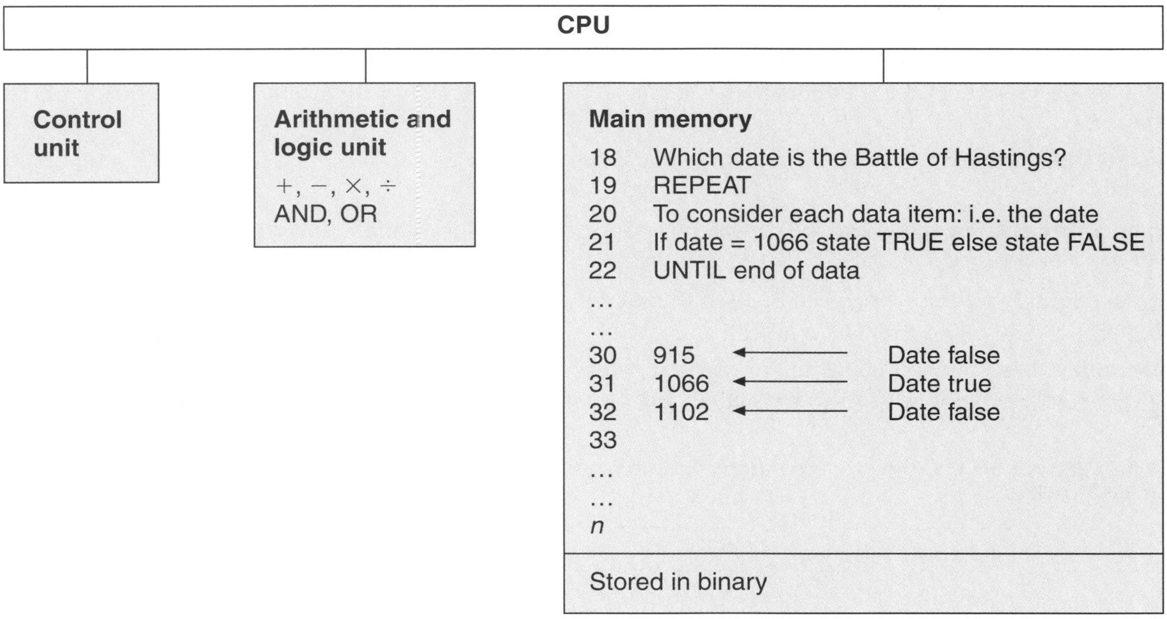

CPU

Control unit

Arithmetic and logic unit

+, −, ×, ÷
AND, OR

Main memory

18 Which date is the Battle of Hastings?
19 REPEAT
20 To consider each data item: i.e. the date
21 If date = 1066 state TRUE else state FALSE
22 UNTIL end of data
...
...
30 915 ← Date false
31 1066 ← Date true
32 1102 ← Date false
33
...
...
n

Stored in binary

Note The information given above is not the actual instructions but a pseudo-code format to help explain what is happening in the program.

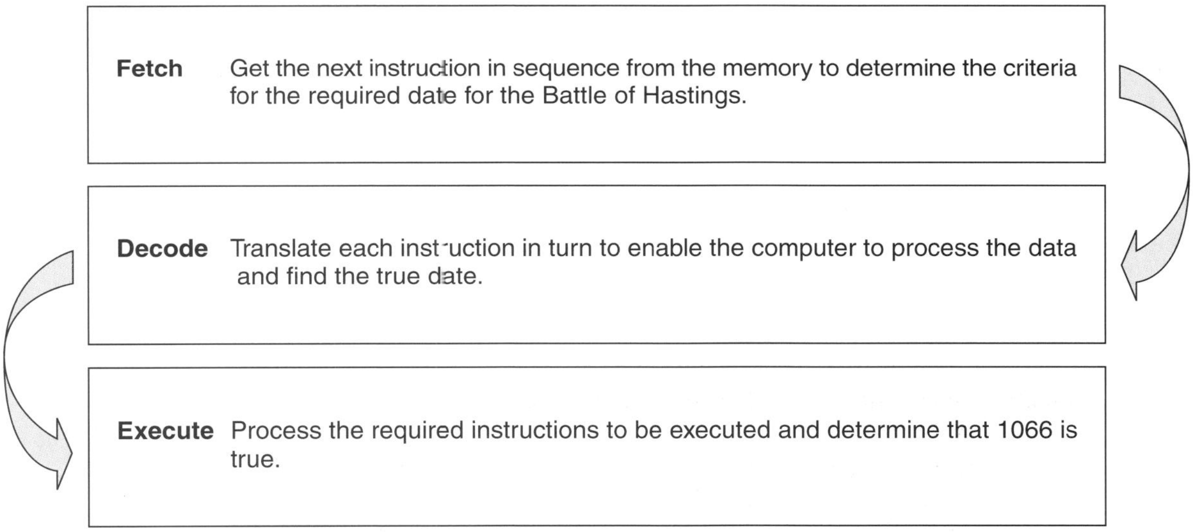

Fetch Get the next instruction in sequence from the memory to determine the criteria for the required date for the Battle of Hastings.

Decode Translate each instruction in turn to enable the computer to process the data and find the true date.

Execute Process the required instructions to be executed and determine that 1066 is true.

Note These operations are carried out one at a time. That is, line 18 fetched – decoded – executed, then line 19, then line 20 and so on.

The program will eventually conclude that 1066 was in fact the year in which the Battle of Hastings was fought.

Interrupts

It is not unusual for the fetch–execute cycle to be interrupted on a fairly regular basis. In such a case, an interrupt routine is activated by the **kernel** (the controlling part of the operating system) to assess the nature of the break in execution.

Types of interrupts

Power failure This is the most serious and is therefore given the highest priority. When a power failure occurs, the kernel attempts to save as much information as it can so that the operation can resume when the power is restored.

Hardware malfunctioning This is a serious interrupt: for example, disc head crash, parity error or circuit board malfunction.

Program/software interrupts These are caused by a range of faults: for example, division by zero, under/overflow detection, incorrect program calls.

Timer interrupts The system clock can be used to interrupt operations at regular intervals. This would facilitate time sharing on a network system.

I/O interrupts These can be deliberate (for example, pressing the ESC/BREAK key) or they could be due to the device being unable to return the correct signal to the processor. The priority level associated with I/O interrupts is low.

When an interrupt occurs, the processor polls the interrupt vector to assess the priority and nature of the problem.

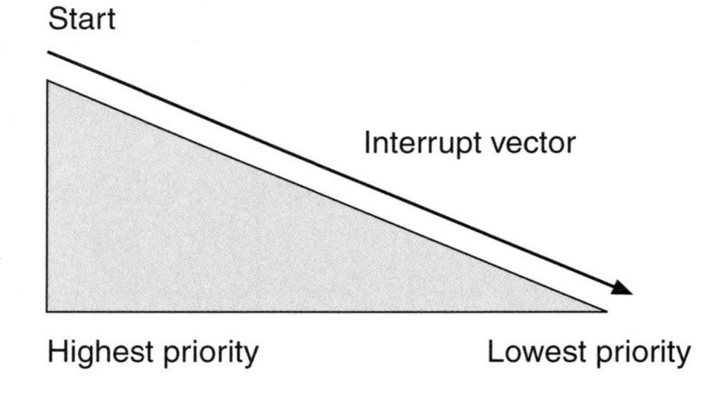

If possible, a message is generated for the user giving the source of the interrupt.

Computer performance

The performance of a computer is affected in several ways:

Word length This refers to the group of bits that are processed as a single unit. The word size is determined by the width of the data lines and is the major factor in assessing the speed of the processor.

Bus size This refers to the width of the bus lines and determines the maximum number of bits that can be processed simultaneously.

Hardware configuration The components used to perform the various operations have an effect on each other. Since the motherboard, sound card, graphics card, memory unit etc, all work in conjunction with each other, they are limited by the slowest or least efficient device.

Clock speed The higher the clock rate, the faster the computer may perform. However, the components used may help or hinder the eventual performance

Pipelining This is the process used to speed up the fetch–execute cycle by fetching a few instructions at once and putting them into a queue so that they can be fed into the CIR more quickly.

Processing concepts

Machine code is the language of the computer. It is in binary format, which means that machine instructions can be executed immediately without being translated into any other format.

Each machine code instruction consists of two distinct parts:

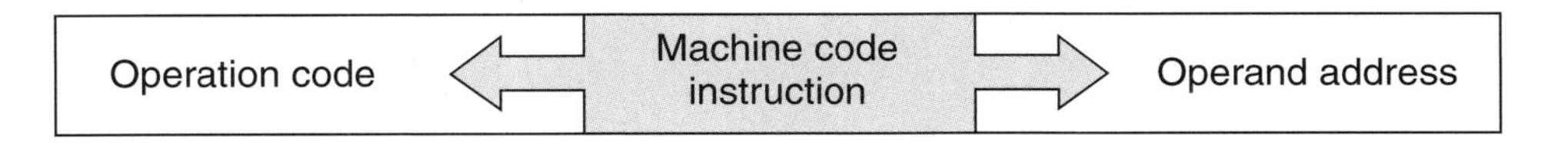

However, there is a number of ways this configuration can be arranged with relation to the number of bits used for each part. If 16 bits were allocated to the operation code, then this would allow 2^{16} different operations.

The lowest level of coding is machine code. However, there are other low-level languages such as **assembly language**. Assembly language uses mnemonic codes and these are mapped one-to-one with an equivalent machine code. For example:

STA #32 Store the value 32 in the accumulator.
Would be used in place of 00001011/00100000.

Quite often three-letter mnemonics are used as an abbreviated format to help the programmer to write low-level programs faster and with fewer errors.

Assembly language instructions have the same format as machine code. That is, they consist of two parts, the operation code and the operand address. This configuration allows for a variety of instruction formats. Five examples are given below.

Three address instruction format

Operation code	A1	A2	A3

This format is rarely if ever used today. It would, however, allow calculations to be carried out and stored easily. For example: ADD 5, 3, ×.

Two address instruction format

Operation code	A1	A2

This format allows for a greater number of bits in each address. It could perform the instruction ADD 3, 4 by putting 3 in A1 and 4 in A2, then the result 3 + 4 into A2, since the result is the important part of the sum.

One and a half instruction format

Operation code	A1	A2

This format allows for a range of addresses to be referenced using many bits in A1. Then probably A2, using for example three bits, could refer to a set of registers to store values.

One address instruction format

Operation code	A1

Instructions, such as LDA 3, STA#4, can be easily implemented using this format. If the instructions were 16 bits long, 6 bits could be used for the operation code giving 2^6 different operations and 10 bits for the address, providing 2^{10} different address locations to be referenced.

Zero address instruction format

Operation code

This allows for instructions which require no address: for example, HLT (Halt) or CLC (Clear the carry bit).

Addressing methods

There are a variety of addressing methods which can be used in assembly language. The most common ones are:

Direct addressing This is where the data in the operand is used as the address location in memory. For example, LDX 12 (this is an address): load the contents of location 12 into the X register.

10		
11		
12	HELLO	

Indirect addressing This is where the data in the operand refers to an address where the required data is stored. For example, LDX 7 (this is an address): move to location 7.

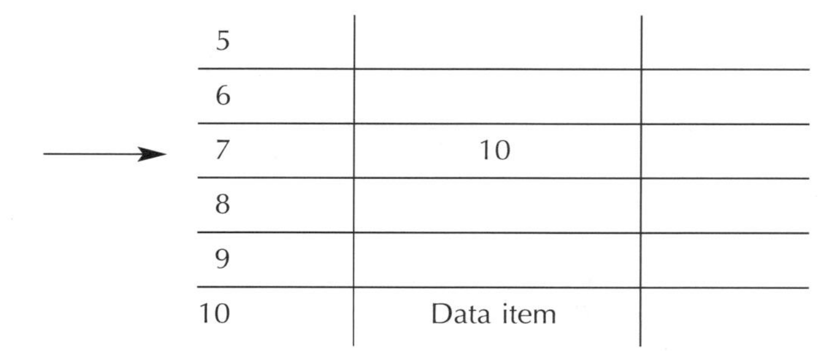

5		
6		
7	10	
8		
9		
10	Data item	

This points to another address at location 10. Get the data from location 10.

Immediate addressing This is where the operand contains the data to be used in the operation. For example, STA#20 (this is a value): store the value 20 in the accumulator.

Indexed addressing This is where the required address is found by adding the value in the operand to a number stored in the index register.

LDA (IR + 9) Move to location 100 + 9 = 109

IR = 100

Base register addressing This is where the base address is held in a register and the operand gives a value which is added to the base value to provide the required address.

Base address XXXXXXXXX

Go to the base address and move from this location by the given number of places to the required address.

Different types of instruction

There are four types of instruction: **arithmetic, logical, branch** and **shift**.

Arithmetic

These instructions include adding, subtracting, multiplying and dividing. There is a variety of different addressing methods which can be used to deal with these operations. Large and small, positive and negative values can be dealt with using, for example, one's and two's complements.

Logical

These instructions include AND and OR. For example, a mask can be used to identify a single bit or group of bits.

a

10110110	Register
	AND
10000000	Mask
10000000	Result

Note When AND is used, only 1 AND 1 will return 1. So, with AND:

$0 + 0 \rightarrow 0$
$0 + 1 \rightarrow 0$
$1 + 0 \rightarrow 0$
$1 + 1 \rightarrow 1$

The mask used enables a single bit to be identified.

10110110	Register
	AND
11110000	Mask
10110000	Result

Note The leftmost four values of the register are found by applying the mask shown above.

The mask used enables a group of bits to be identified.

b

1001	Register
	OR
0101	Mask
1101	Result

Note When OR is used, every combination except 0 OR 0 will return 1. So, with OR:

$0 + 0 \rightarrow 0$
$0 + 1 \rightarrow 1$
$1 + 0 \rightarrow 1$
$1 + 1 \rightarrow 1$

c If X = 1100
and Y = 1010
LDA X: load 1100 into accumulator
AND Y: perform a logical AND operation

This will place the result of X AND Y into the accumulator.

Branch

These instructions change the sequence in which the instructions are carried out. There are two main types:

Conditional If condition is met – for example, BNE (branch if result not equal to zero) or BNZ (branch if result is equal to zero) – then the program will be executed from a new position.

Unconditional In this type of instruction, the jump will always occur: for example, JP 200 (jump to location 200).

Shift

There are three main types of shift instruction. They are used to manipulate the values within a register.

Logical shifts

These are LSR (logical shift right) and LSL (logical shift left). With this method, the bits in a register are moved a given number of places to the left or right. Since the register is of fixed size, any bits moving beyond its region are lost.

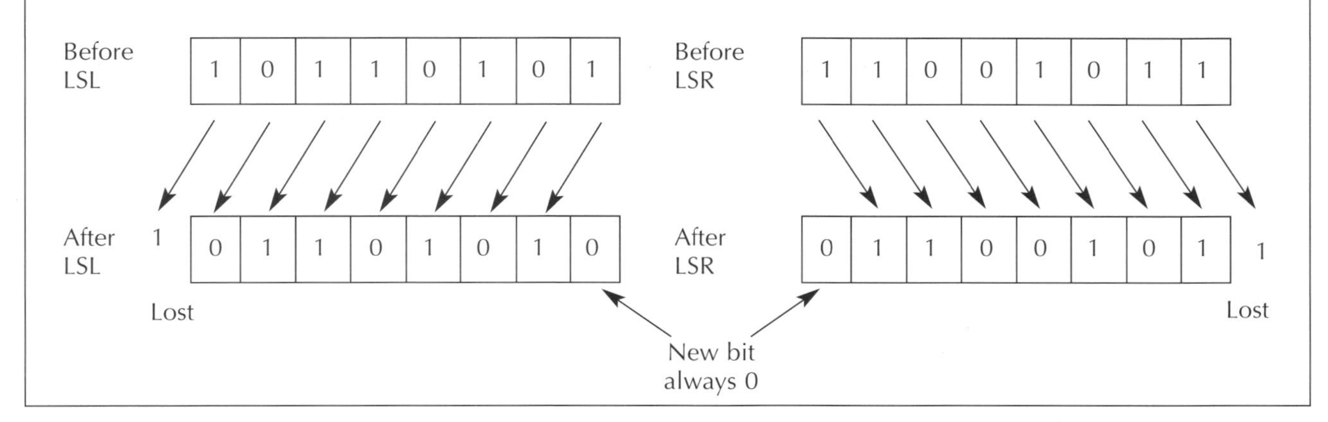

Different types of instruction (continued)

Cyclic shift

This is where the bits fall off one end of the register and reappear on the other. Examples of CSR (cyclic shift right) and CSL (cyclic shift left) are shown below.

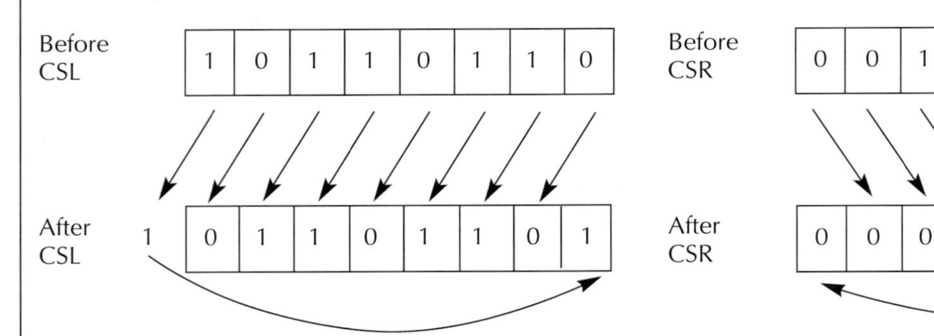

Arithmetic shift

With this method, the sign bits are fixed and the other bits in the register move to the left or right. Examples of ASL (arithmetic shift left) and ASR (arithmetic shift right) are shown below.

- When the sign bit (shaded grey) is negative, that is set to 1:

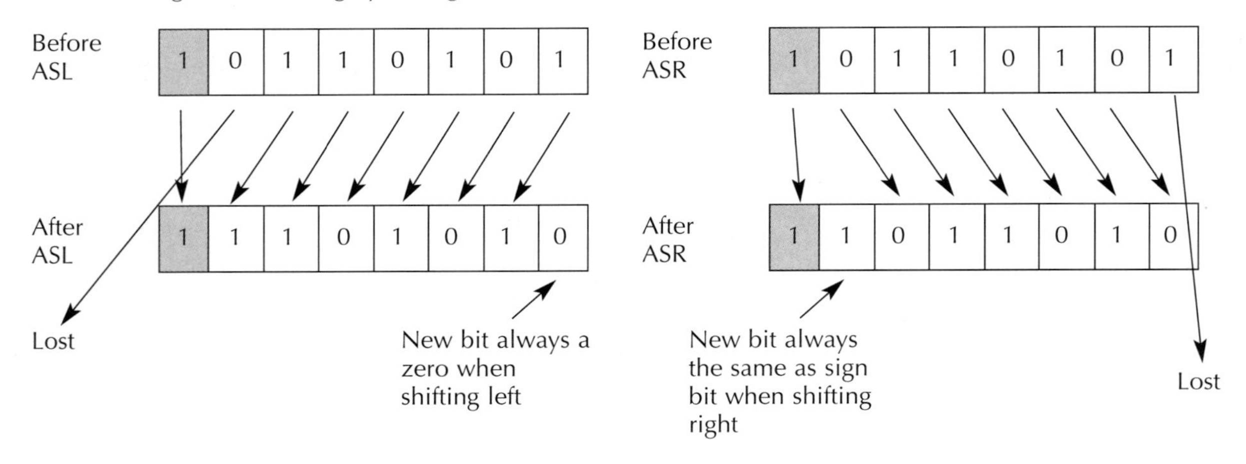

- When the sign bit (shaded grey) is positive, that is set to 0:

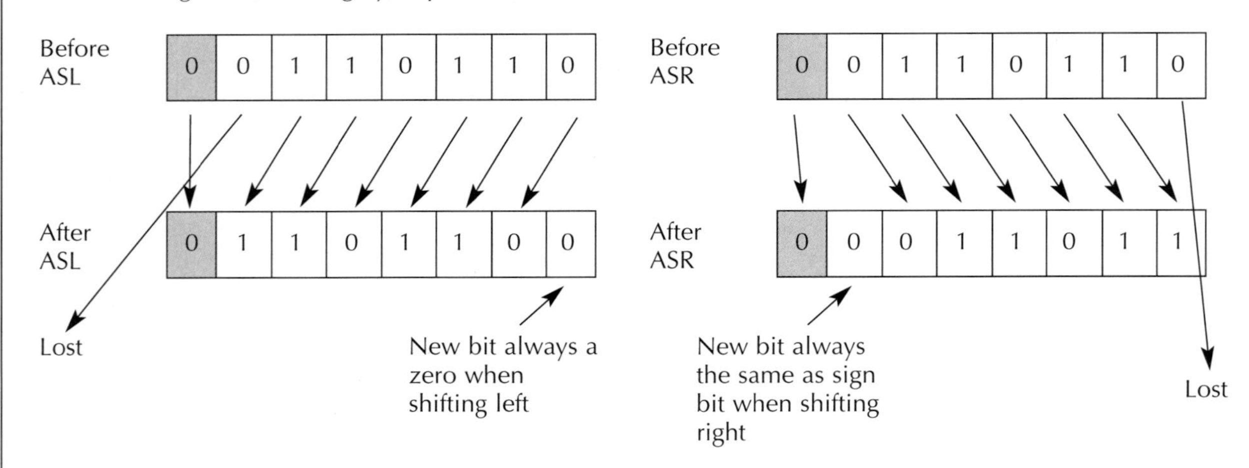

Arithmetic shifting to the left represents multiplication by 2 on the register value, and shifting to the right division by 2. The limiting factor is the register size. For example, with 8 bits:

Maximum positive value $2^7 - 1$ Minimum value -2^7

Values outside this range cause overflow or underflow errors.

Other assembly language key terms

Macro instruction
This is where a single instruction triggers a group of instructions. When the macro is called, the group of instructions are used at that point.

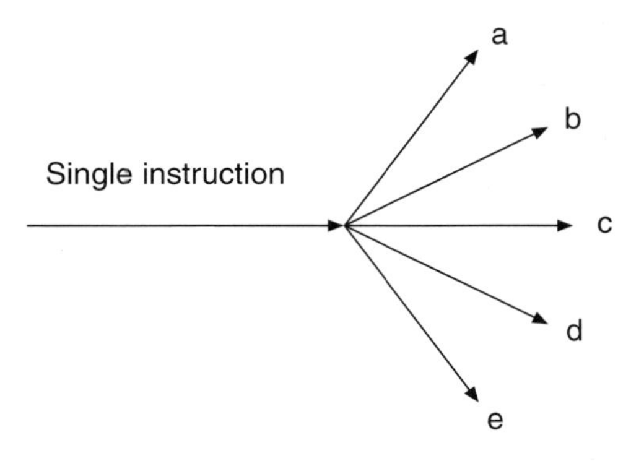

Directive
These are instructions which are acted on immediately. Although they are used in assembly code, they do not require translation into machine code. For example:

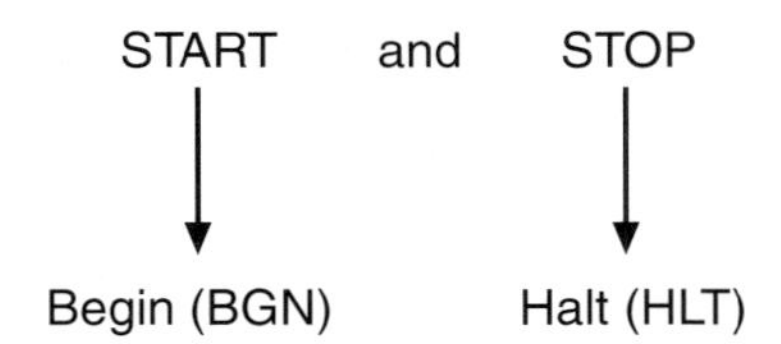

High-level language characteristics

The wide selection of high-level languages (HLLs) now available were all designed to meet the needs of specific problems.

HLL statements are close to English and therefore the readability of the system is easier to understand and change. Debugging the programs is also easier due to the meaningful variable names and user comments that can be used. Some languages provide a wide variety of mathematical precision and handle basic mathematical expressions with ease.

HLL are portable thus enabling users to run the programs on a variety of platforms provided the necessary software is present to meet the platform requirements.

The main disadvantages of HLLs are the speed of execution (which is slow compared with low-level languages) and the size of the translated machine program (which is lengthy compared with the assembly or machine programs).

High-level languages

BASIC (Beginners All-purpose Symbolic Instruction Code)
This language was developed to help to teach programming. The language is very popular today, especially with microcomputer users. Microsoft have developed a product based on BASIC called **Visual Basic**. It is object-oriented and makes full use of the GUI.

COBOL (Common Business Oriented Language)
This is an extremely popular language, which is used extensively in commercial and business applications. Each COBOL program consists of four divisions:

1. Identification: title, date, etc
2. Environment: hardware requirements
3. Data: data structure and types identified
4. Procedure: program instructions

Pascal
This language was designed to teach programming. It encourages good design and clear structure. Pascal is still widely used today in many schools, colleges and universities.

FORTRAN (FORmula TRANslation)
This was developed for use in scientific and engineering applications. Fortran was the first high-level language and was used extensively to produce programming solutions to scientific and mathematical problems. Calculations can be performed with a high degree of accuracy and the availability of a large set of mathematical functions makes it particularly suitable for scientific applications.

C
This is the benchmark program in terms of speed. C is used in the development of systems programs and in applications where speed is an essential criterion, such as real-time systems.

Java
This is the most popular language in the world. Java is extremely robust, making it the ideal solution for running programs on single computers or on networked machines. It is a platform-independent program, extensively used on the World Wide Web.

PROLOG (PROgramming LOGic)
PROLOG is well suited to work carried out with expert systems and artificial intelligence. It does this by declaring facts, asking questions and defining rules about a certain area of knowledge.

In medicine, knowledge about specific parts of the body can be gathered from a wide variety of recognised and reliably tested sources. This core of knowledge can then be interrogated to help diagnose symptoms pertaining to that body part and even suggest possible treatments. This is known as an **expert system.**

Programming features

Selection structures

This type of statement allows a selection to be made within a high-level language program. If a certain condition is true, then do something. If not, do something else.

The examples given use the 'If … then … (ELSE)' statement.

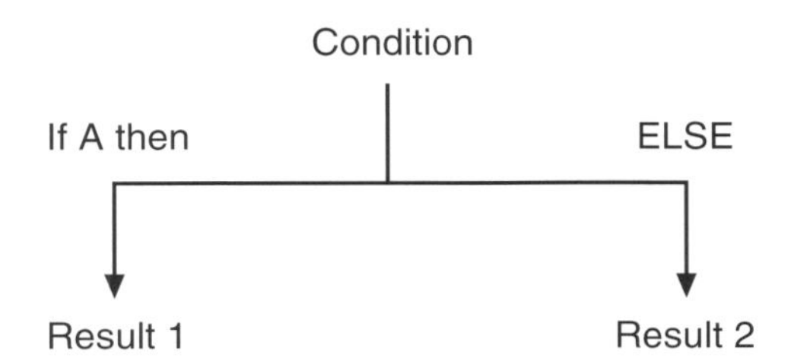

For example, if your score in a test is over 50, you pass the test. If not, you have failed.

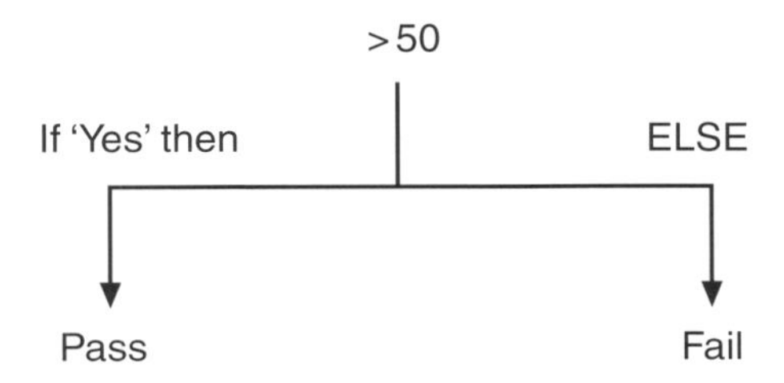

Depending on the high-level language being used, the system will differ slightly, but the basic selection concept remains.

If the condition has many options, then the **case element** can be used,

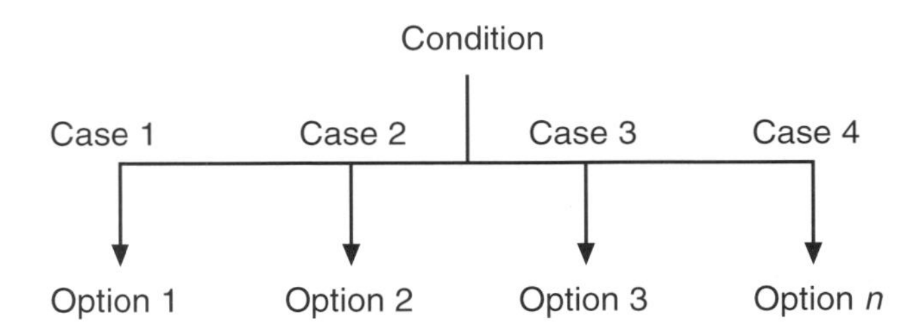

where *n* can represent any number of possible outcomes.

For example, if your test score is over 50, you pass. If it is over 60, you get a commendation. If it is over 75, you get a distinction. Otherwise, you fail.

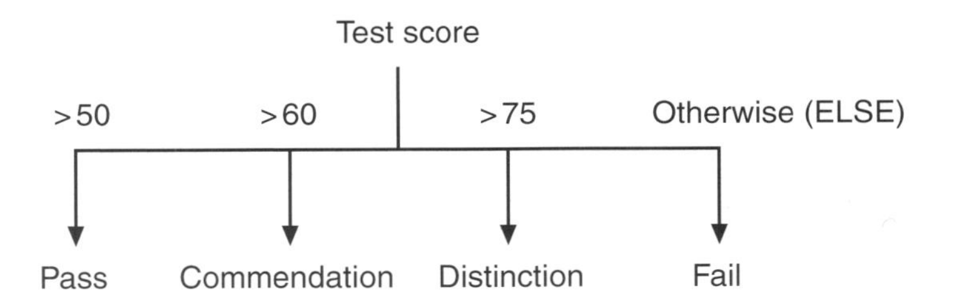

Programming features (continued)

Iterative structures

High-level programming languages provide a number of ways to repeat a sequence of instructions in the form of a loop.

While loop	END WHILE While number > 0
While a condition is true, a sequence of instructions is executed. When the condition is false, the loop is exited.	**Note** The condition is at the start and therefore the loop will only be activated if the number is greater than zero.

This loop structure is used when the number of iterations is unknown. The loop will not be executed even once if the false condition is encountered first.

Repeat Until loop	UNTIL CONDITION TRUE Repeat
Repeat a set of instructions until a condition is met. This loop will keep repeating until the condition is true.	**Note** The condition is at the end, therefore the loop will always be executed at least once.

This loop structure is used when the number of iterations is unknown. Sometimes a rogue value is used with Repeat . . . Until and While loops. For example, a loop could be repeated until the value entered was 9999, after which the loop would terminate. This rogue value would not be one of the normally expected values and so would only be used to stop the loop.

For . . . Next loop

This loop is executed a fixed number of times. The number of iterations can be represented by a constant (for example 10), or a variable which has been assigned a value earlier in the program. For example:

```
FOR I = 1 to 10              FOR I = 1 to total
_______________      or      _______________
_______________              _______________
_______________              _______________
_______________              _______________
NEXT                         NEXT
```

This loop structure is used when the number of iterations is known beforehand.

Assignment statements

This facility enables the programmer to have control over the variables used and the results they produce. For example:

Volume = Length × Width × Height

This statement tells the computer to multiply the values length, width and height together and place the result into a memory location called Volume.

Number : = Number + 1

Mathematically this does not make much sense! But, when it is understood to be an assignment statement, it can be handled.

It basically reads as follows:

Get the existing value of the memory location called Number and add 1 to it. Then place the new result back into the memory location called Number. Therefore, if the number was 4 before this statement, it will now be 5.

Subprograms

In a data processing environment, it is much easier to write computer programs if they are split up into small manageable units rather than treated as one large program. The two main types of subprogram are called **Procedures** and **Functions**.

Programming features (continued)

Procedures

Procedures are used extensively in HLL, and can be written and tested independently of the rest of the program. Procedures can be written to carry out just about any programming task and can be reused in other programs if written independently of the main program.

It is good practice in computer programming to give meaningful variable and procedure names. A procedure is 'called' by writing its name, and this is much easier to work with and remember if it has some resemblance to what the subprogram is designed to do. For example:

Procedure: Draw rectangle

____

____

____

The program draws a rectangle on the screen.

____

____

____

End the procedure.

Procedures are quite often written using variables called **parameters**, which help to customise the code to perform in a certain way for different situations. For example, a procedure could be written to draw a rectangle but the actual starting point and the length and width could be included.

Define Procedure: Draw rectangle (*x, y, length, width*)

When the procedure is called, these variables will be given actual values.

Procedure: Draw rectangle

(100, 200, 500, 300)

x *y* L W

The above shows that 100 goes into *x*, 200 into *y*, 500 into length, 300 into width.

Note It is important that these values (parameters) match the order in the Procedure definition

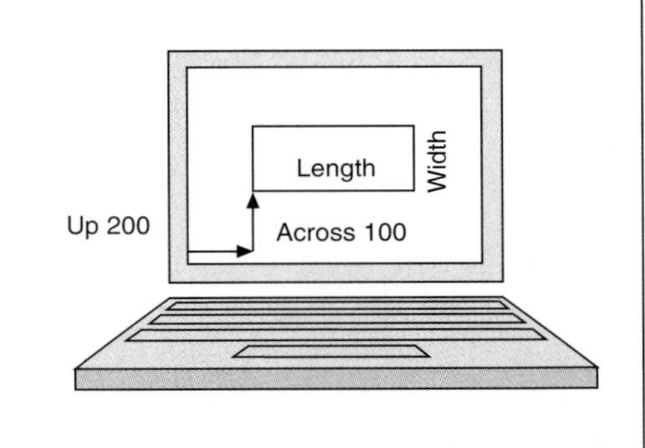

Using parameters, this rectangle can be located anywhere on the screen and be drawn to any size that is within the screen restrictions.

Functions

A function is similar to a procedure but is usually used to return a value. For example:

Function: Area of circle

____

____

Get the radius

____

____

Area pi × radius × radius

____

____

Display the value of Area

____

____

End the Function

Programming features (continued)

Built-in features

Many HLLs have functions which are built-in to enable the user to make full use of the programming environment. These may include: using a random number generator; finding the square root of a number; finding the remainder of a division sum.

Data structures used in HLLs allow programmers to manage large amounts of data easily and to manipulate the data as a single unit. Examples of data structures are: arrays, trees, lists, strings and files.

Some HLLs have built-in routines to facilitate the manipulation of data. In Pascal, for example, readin and writein are used with inputting and outputting data.

Block structure, local and global variables

Most HLLs have a set structure which has to be adhered to. Pascal is an example of a block-structured language because of the way the code has to be presented.

The Pascal block structure has two main sections:

Declaration section This may comprise some or all of the following: program name; data; variables; constant and label declarations; data type definitions, procedures and functions.

Main program section This may comprise of one or more subblocks.

Global variables have significance and relevance throughout the entire program

Local variables are defined only for use within one section of the program. This is usually restricted to a Procedure or Function

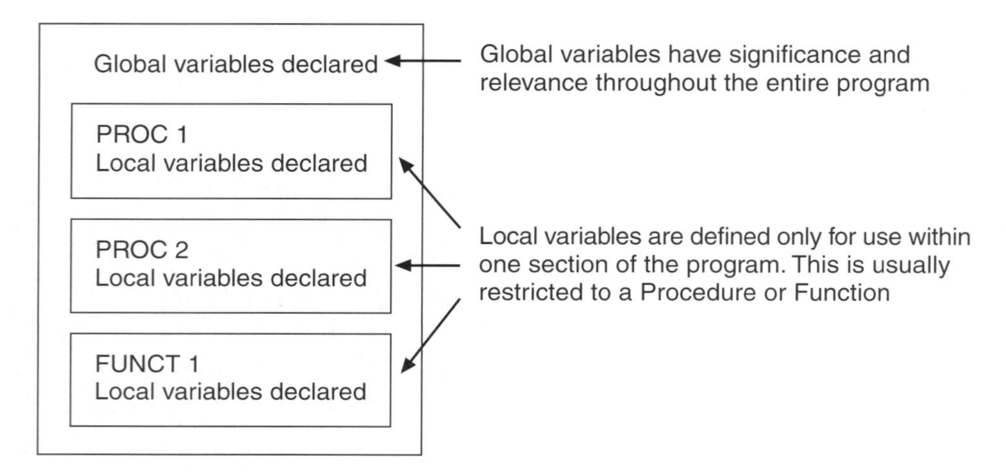

Recursion

In a computing context, recursion usually refers to a situation when a subprogram calls itself. It is important to know that when any subprogram is called, the return address is automatically pushed onto the stack (so that the program can continue from where it left off once the subprogram has ended).

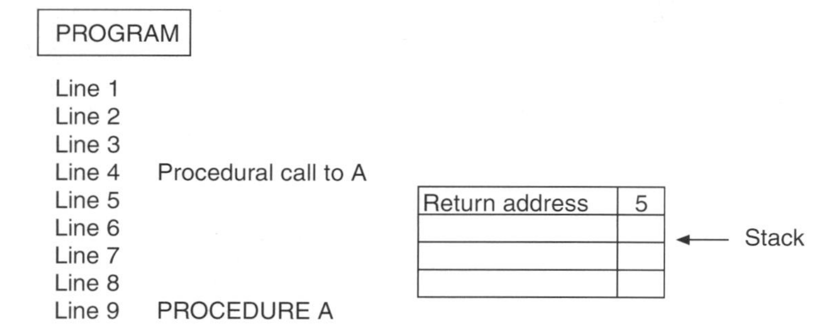

When the program jumps to the procedure at Line 4, the stack stores the address of the next line of code for the return.

Language categories

Computer languages can be categorised in a number of different ways, one of which is by generation:

First generation language – Machine code
Second generation language – Assembly code
Third generation languages – BASIC, Pascal, COBOL, FORTRAN
Fourth generation language – Structured query language (SQL)

The main distinguishing rule is that the higher the generation gets, the closer it gets to the natural language in English. Also, the higher the generation, the more translation is needed to convert it into machine code.

Another way of categorising languages is by type, as given below.

Imperative or procedural languages
Most conventional HLLs are of this type, in that code is used to tell the computer how to do a specific task using commands.

A sequence of instructions are written by the programmer and the computer carries them out in the strict order specified in the program. Examples of imperative languages are BASIC, Pascal, COBOL and FORTRAN.

Declarative languages
With this type of language, problems are represented in terms of objects and the relationships they have with one another. By declaring facts, asking questions (or queries) and defining rules, declarative languages such as PROLOG can be used to great effect. This language type focuses in on 'What to do' rather than 'How to do' it. For example, these facts could be keyed:

Male (Ian – Simons)
Is – a (Ian – Simons, fine – musician)
Is – a (Ian – Simons, pop – icon)
Is – a (Ian – Simons, superb – sportsman)
Is – a (Tober – dog)

The first fact states that Ian Simons is male and the last fact states that Tober is a dog, which are true. However, the other facts are just wishful thinking on the part of the author. (Even computers can give the wrong information if fed with the wrong input data.)

But if this query were typed in:

? is – a (Ian – Simons, fine – musician)

In other words

Is Ian Simons a fine musician?

PROLOG would return the answer 'Yes'.

Object-oriented languages
With this type of language, objects, such as data structures are identified and operations are performed on them. Languages such as C++, Java, Delphi and Visual Basic are called object-oriented because the programmer can select an object and manipulate the data items linked with it.

In Visual Basic, the toolbox contains a set of icons which when selected allows the user to place a new object into a form. The property editor is a list of characteristics or properties which affect the currently selected object. By changing the properties, the user controls the appearance of the object.

Key concepts

Encapsulation
Each object has a set of properties which are attached to it. This attachment is referred to as **encapsulation**. It follows then, that if the data structure or the function of an object is to be altered, this can be easily done and need not affect other parts of the program. Programs written in this way are faster and more efficient in terms of modifying, updating, testing and maintaining.

Object classes and subclasses
An object is a member of a class if it possesses certain characteristics which are exhibited by the other objects in that class. For example, lecturers at a university are objects because they have common attributes – they work at the university, they give lectures to students, and so on.

Note At a university there may be other groups of lecturers who have other duties in addition to lecturing: for example, part-time staff who may also work in business or research. These additional categories are subclasses of the main lecturers' class.

Inheritance
Once an object has been created, subclasses can be established which share the main characteristics of the original. This process of possessing shared features is called **inheritance**.

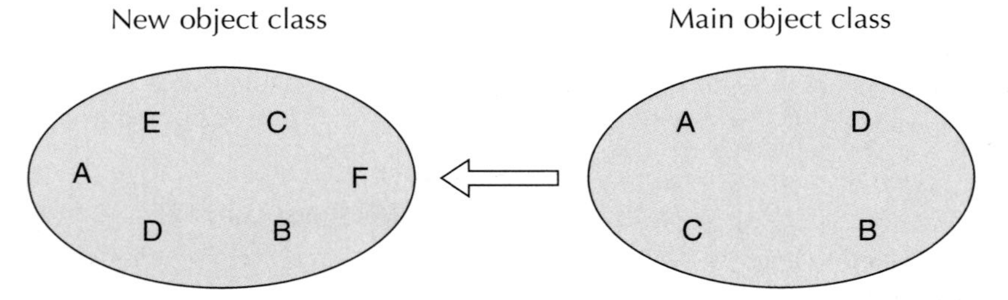

Characteristics A, B, C and D have been inherited from the main object class.

Polymorphism
This refers to a situation where two or more objects share common characteristics but each still contain unique ones of its own.

Containment
This occurs when an object class is contained within another class. Rather like a set and a subset in mathematics.

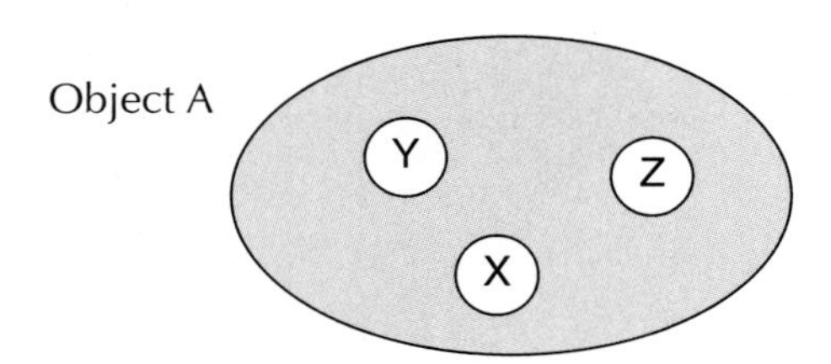

Objects X, Y and Z are contained in Object A.

Event-driven programming
In object-oriented programming, objects can be created which respond to a particular event taking place. For example, a command button object in Visual Basic can be activated by clicking on it. The code is written and the event only takes place when the pointer is over the object and the mouse is clicked or the enter key is pressed on the keyboard.

Command button

When the pointer is over the object and the mouse is clicked, a set of program instructions are automatically carried out.

Translation software

Assembler

Source code | Translator | Object code

Assembly language → Assembler → Machine code

Low-level language | Low-level language

Example:

LDA screen
CNF #1
STX
→
10111011
10110111
0110011

Assembler
- A piece of systems software
- Converts each assembly language source code statement into a machine code statement prior to executing it
- Each assembly instruction has an equivalent machine code instruction
- A copy of the source code and object code programs are stored
- Assemblers are machine specific

Assembly processes

One-pass assembler

- The assembler converts the mnemonic source code into machine code in one sweep of the program.
- This type of assembler cannot handle code which involves forward referencing.

Two-pass assembler

The problems with the previous type of assembler are overcome with this type.

- On the fast pass:
  - A symbol table is created to enter symbolic addresses and labels into specific addresses.
  - All errors are suppressed.
- On the second pass:
  - The jump instructions can access the memory addresses from the table.
  - The whole source code is translated into machine code.
  - Errors are reported, if they exist.

Interpreter

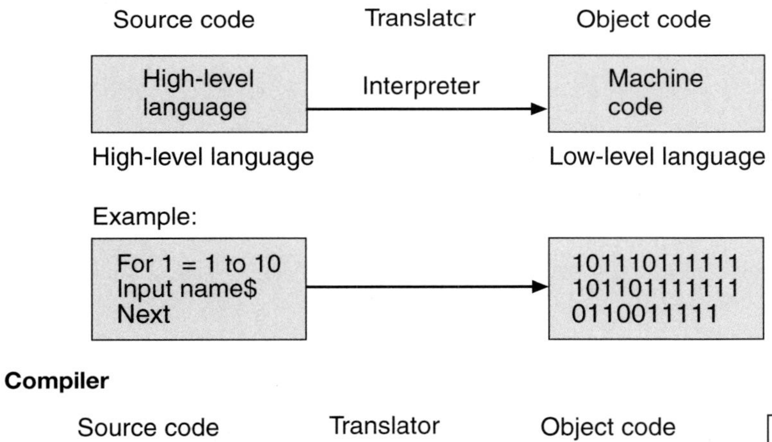

Interpreter
- A piece of systems software
- Converts each high-level language instruction line by line into machine code
- Retranslates the source code each time it is run
- Ideal for debugging (taking errors out of) the program

Compiler

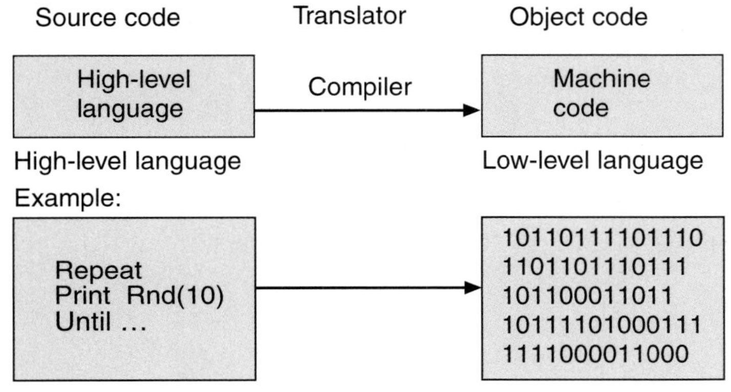

Compiler
- A piece of systems software
- Each high-level language instruction is converted into many machine code instructions
- The compiler saves a copy of the source code and object code programs
- Converts each high-level language instruction into machine code before executing it

Translation software (continued)

Stages of compilation

The compiler is a very complex program. The process by which the high-level language instructions are translated into machine code can be explained in several stages.

1 Lexical analysis

- Keywords used in the source language are replaced with **tokens** (unique shortened codes).
- Any identifying names that the programmer has used are put into a **symbol table** for easy reference.
- All spaces and programmer comments are removed during this phase to help to make the code as compact as possible
- The code is checked by the lexical analyser for simple errors and, if any exist, an error report is generated.

2 Syntax analysis

- A detailed check of the input tokens is made to determine if they are grammatically correct (that is, not violating the rules of the language). This process is carried out by the parser and can therefore be called **parsing**.
- A semantic analysis may be carried out to determine if the meaning of tokenised statements are acceptable.
- A **dictionary** is generated to store information about variables used in the program.

3 Code generation

- Each parsed instruction is converted into machine code.
- Optimisation is carried out to make the program as efficient as possible.
- The machine code program is produced from the optimised code.

Syntax analysis diagrams

The syntax of a language refers to the rules that govern it. A convenient method for expressing these rules is by using syntax diagrams. For example, an identifier may be defined by

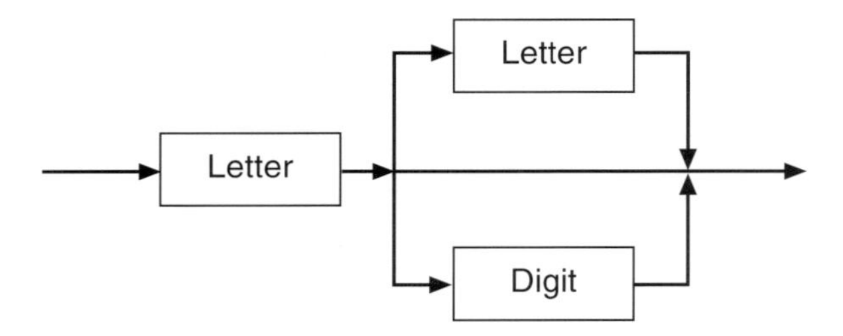

This would mean that the identifier would have to begin with a letter but could have any number of alphanumeric characters after it.

Syntax definition

Strict guidelines are set out when the syntax of a language is being developed. One such method of defining syntax is Backus Naur Form (BNF). This is known as a **meta language** and consists of a set of symbols. For example:

::=	means 'is defined by'
|	means 'or'
<..>	used to define a meta variable

This gives

<letter>	::= a | b| ... | z
<digit>	::= 0 | 1 | 2 | 3 | 4 | 5 | 6 | 7 | 8 | 9

Meta variables can be defined, then linked together to form a more complex set of rules.

Data structures represent the way data is organised, managed and manipulated within a computing environment. The basic data structures are lists, stacks, queues, trees, files, tables and arrays.

Lists

A **list** is a set of data elements stored in order. For example, [Monday, Tuesday, Wednesday, Thursday, Friday, Saturday, Sunday] is a list of days in the week.

Data elements may be added or deleted at any position in the list and may even be repeated. For example, the days a person has to work in the next fortnight might be: [Mon, Tue, Wed, Sun, Mon, Tue, Sat, Sun]. Data elements may also be ordered or searched for.

Note Lists can contain data elements of the same or different data types and can even contain sublists (a list within a list).

Operations on a list

Empty list

For example, an operation to check whether a list is empty or not could be: Empty (List).

This represents a list with no elements in it and is usually denoted by [ ].

The Boolean values of True and False are used to denote if the list is in fact empty or not. If empty then True, otherwise False.

Head and tail

For example, an operation to print the head of a list of colours could be: Head (List).

Where colours = [Green, Red, Black, White].

So, Head ([Green, Red, Black, White]) would return the element Green.

The first element in a list is the Head and the remainder is the Tail.

Note The Head returns a single element while the Tail returns a list.

Therefore, Green is the Head and Red, Black and White are the Tail.

So, the operation to print the Tail of a list of colours could be: Tail (List). That is, Tail ([Green, Red, Black, White]) would give the result Red, Black, White.

These operations can be combined to select individual elements.

For example: Head (Tail (Colours)).

This asks for the Head (that is, the first item) of the Tail (that is, the last three items) and would give the colour Red.

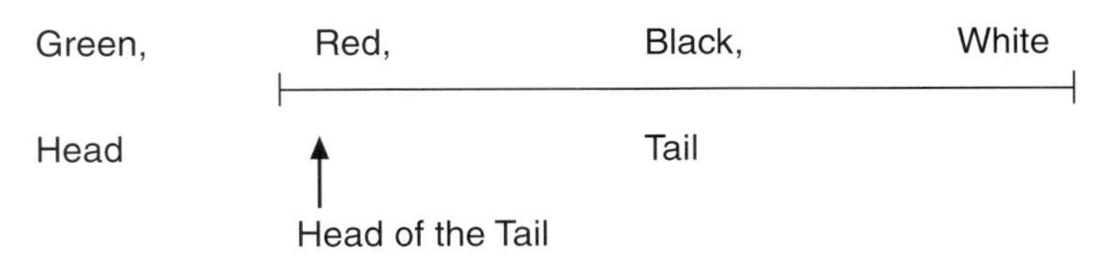

Stacks

A **stack** is a data structure where data elements are added or deleted from the same end. For example:

New names are added to the top and when names are to be deleted, they come from the top.

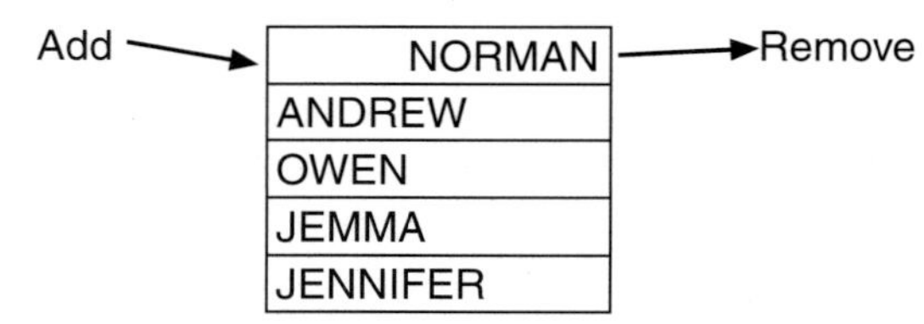

Because of the way elements are added and deleted using a stack, it is referred to as a **lifo** (last in first out) data structure.

Stacks are finite in that they have a limited amount of space for holding data.

Push is the term used to describe adding data elements to a stack. **Pop** is the term used to describe taking data elements off a stack.

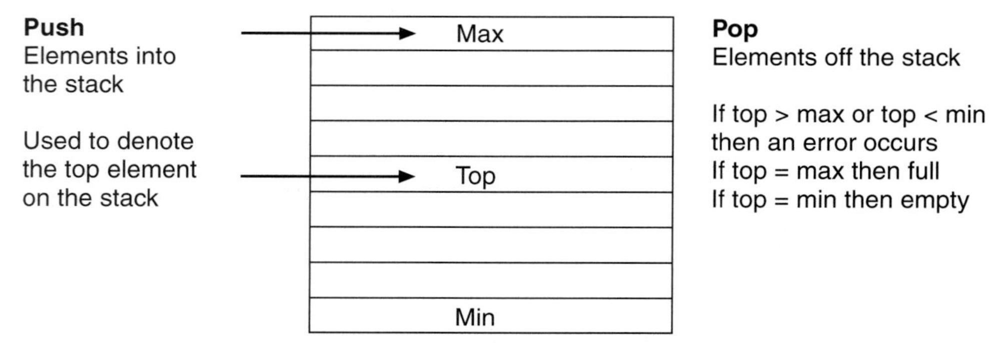

Overflow occurs if one tries to push elements onto a stack that is already full. Underflow occurs if one tries to pop elements off an empty stack.

Stacks can be used very effectively to store return addresses with procedures and subroutines. When the program is being executed and jumps are made to subroutines, the return address is placed on top of the stack and is used when the subroutine ends to resume execution from that address location. Many return addresses can be pushed onto the stack but they are popped off from the top.

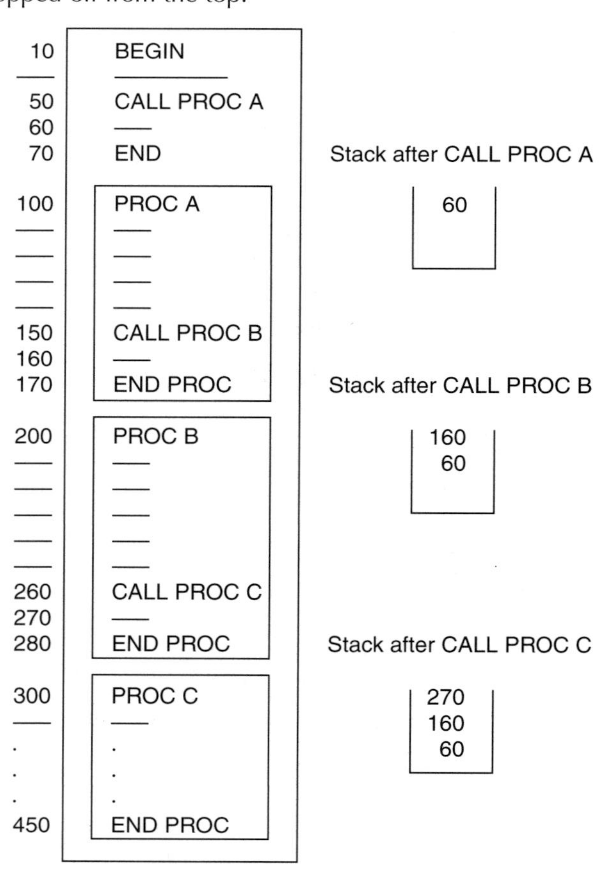

Queues

A queue is a data structure where data elements are added at one end and retrieved from the other.

Rear | Front

Add new elements → | | | | | F | D | X | B | A | Retrieve elements

Due to the nature of data elements entering and leaving the queue, it is referred to as a **fifo** (first in first out) data structure.

Data elements do not actually move along the queue but the front and rear of the queue is denoted by using pointers.

A type of circular list or circular queue is established, because elements do not actually move. Space left by elements that were popped off is used again

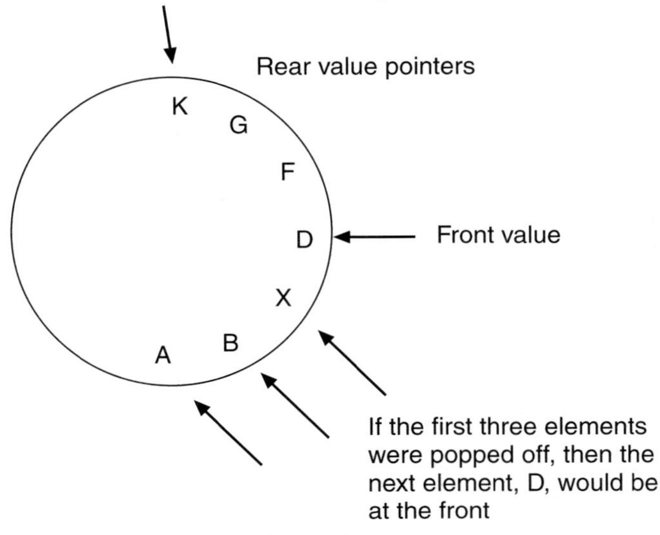

Overflow and underflow occur in the same way as the stack.

Queues are used to store data waiting to be processed by the computer. That is, data can be queued in a printer buffer waiting for printing, or jobs can be placed in a queue waiting for processing.

Binary trees

A **binary tree** is a data structure where data elements are linked to each other in a hierarchical way. Each data element is referred to as a **node** and each node can have at most two descendants (hence binary – base 2).

Note The term 'children' is sometimes used instead of descendants.

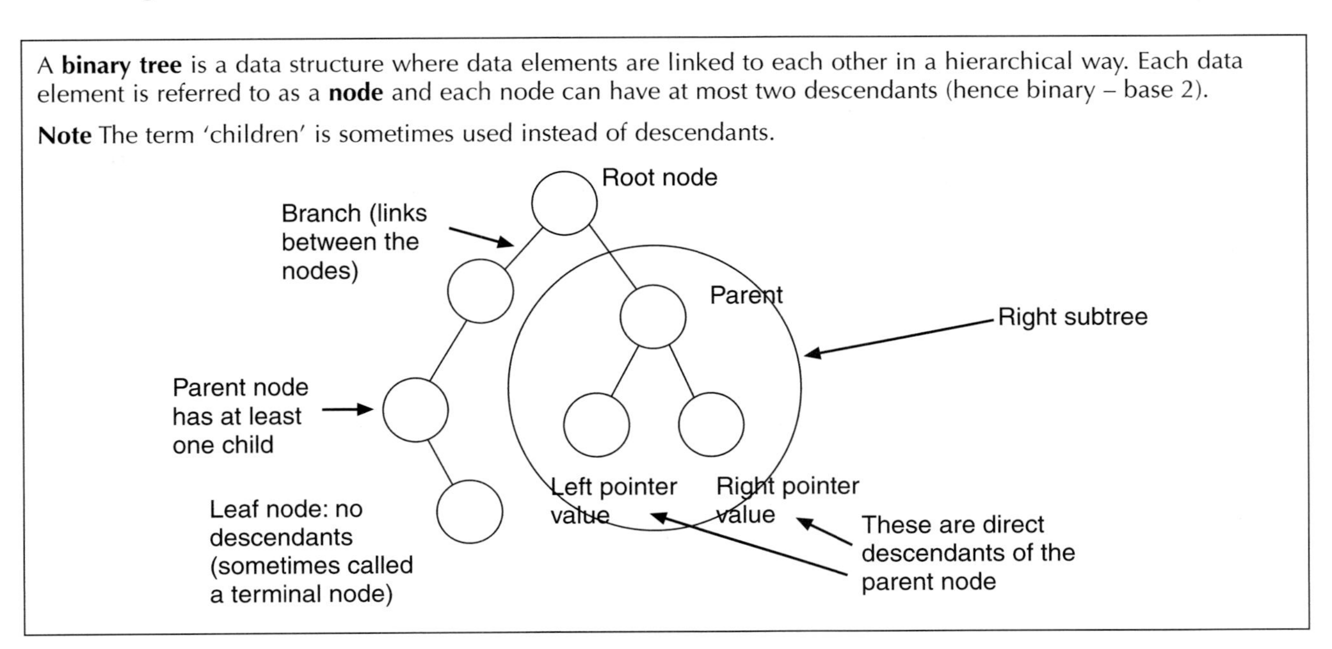

Binary trees (continued)

Tree data structures are manipulated by using pointers and are extensively used when dealing with directories of files (linked with subdirectories).

Binary trees are fairly easy to create. For example, consider the following list of names: Parkinson, Caruth, Simons, Buchanan, Hutchinson, Roberts, Lee, Taylor.

- Place the first element as the root node.
- If the next element is less (alphabetically), place it to the left; otherwise place it on the right.
- New elements can be inserted when an empty leaf node is reached.

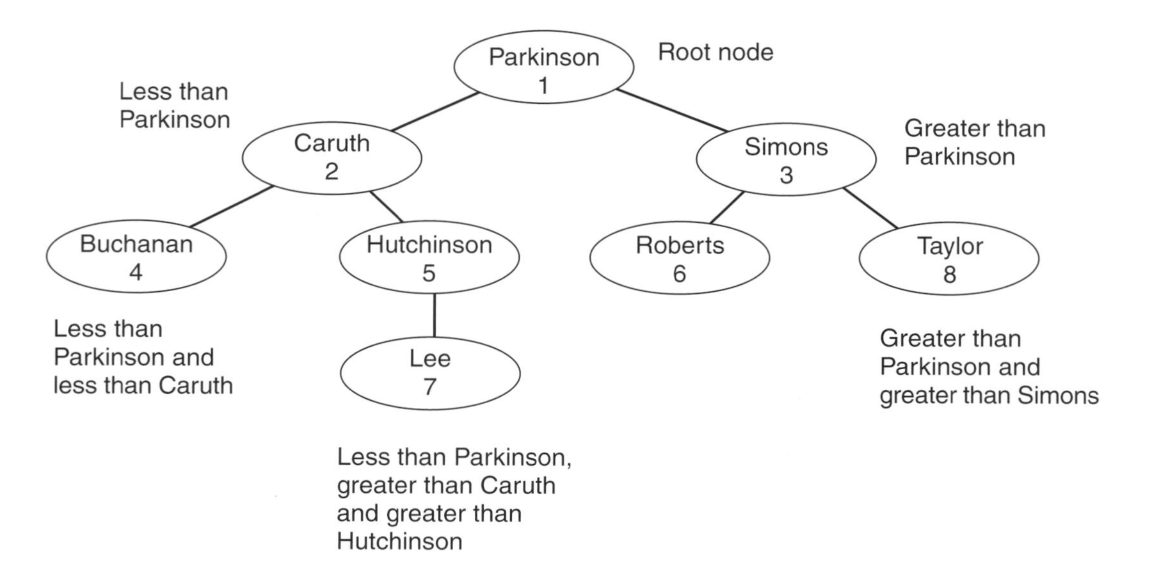

In order to manipulate the elements in the tree, the computer needs to keep track of where the various nodes are pointing to. The following table helps to illustrate this information.

Order number	Left pointer	Element	Right pointer
1	2	Parkinson	3
2	4	Caruth	5
3	6	Simons	8
4	0(−1)	Buchanan	0(−1)
5	0(−1)	Hutchinson	7
6	0(−1)	Roberts	0(−1)
7	0(−1)	Lee	0(−1)
8	0(−1)	Taylor	0(−1)

This table shows that element 1 (Parkinson) points to element 2 (Caruth) on the left and to element 3 (Simons) on the right.

This shows that Taylor has no descendants.

Note 0 or −1 are used to denote no branches. If the left and right pointers are 0, then that node is a leaf node: namely, Buchanan, Lee, Roberts and Taylor.

Deleting nodes from a tree

- To delete a leaf or terminal node (for example, Lee), simply replace the pointer to that node with a 0 or −1, and remove the data. Hence, to delete Lee, replace Hutchinson's right pointer with 0, so 0 Hutchinson 7 becomes 0 Hutchinson 0, and remove the name Lee.
- To delete a node within a tree (for example, Simons), proceed as follows.

Binary trees (continued)

If Simons has a descendant to the left and it, in turn, has descendants, replace Simons with the rightmost element of this left subtree. For example:

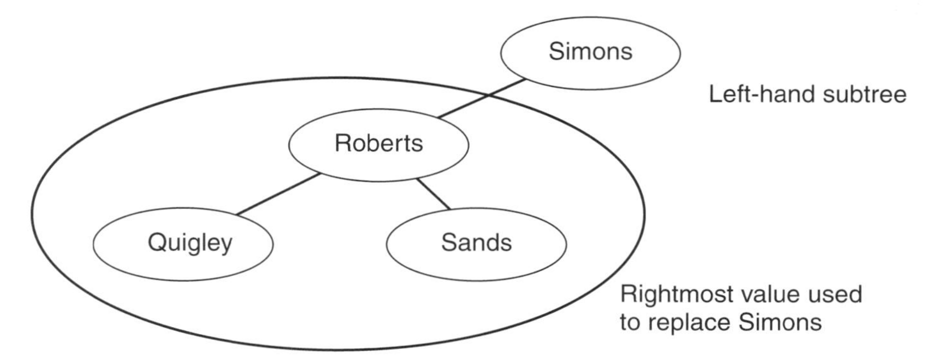

If Simons has only one descendant to the left, replace Simons with this element, as shown below.

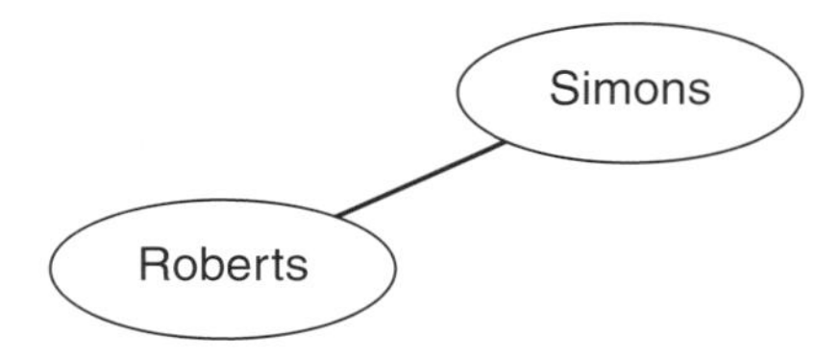

Finally, if Simons has no descendants to the left, replace Simons with the first descendant on the right, as shown below.

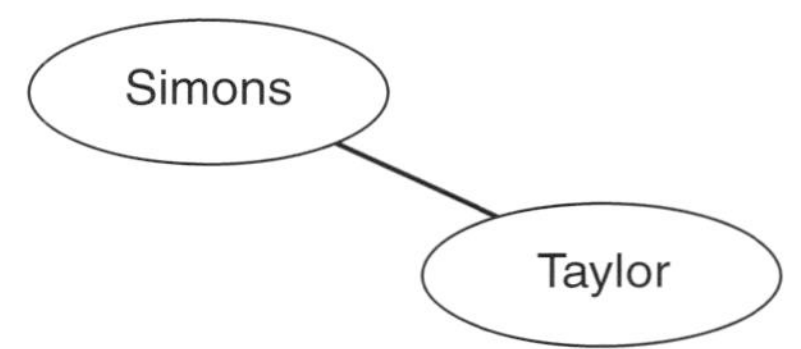

By deleting in this way, the minimum number of changes are made to the table.

Traversing a binary tree

This refers to the order in which the nodes of a tree are visited. Three common traversal routes are: **preorder**, **inorder** and **postorder**. They refer to the occurrence when the root node is to be visited:

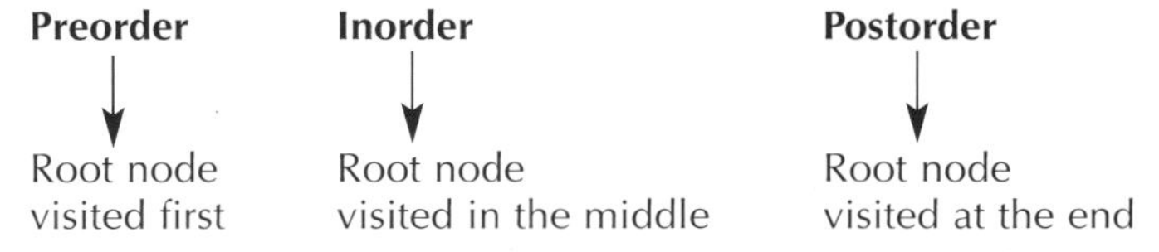

Note The left subtree is *always* visited before the right.

Consider the following binary tree.

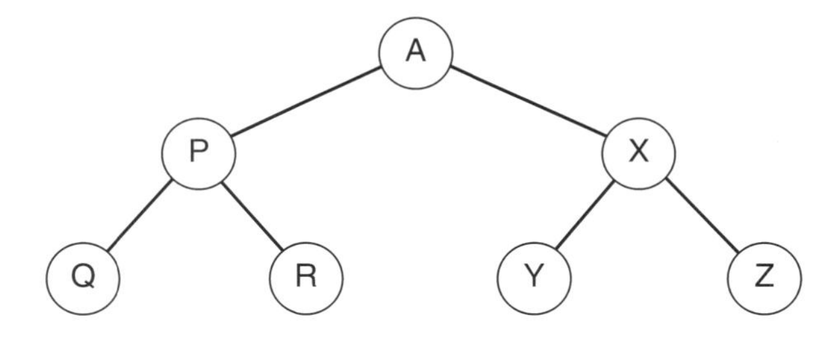

Binary trees (continued)

Formal description for Preorder
- Print the root node data.
- Traverse left subtree (call this recursively until leaf node).
- Traverse right subtree (call this recursively until leaf node).

Preorder
- 1 Begin at the root node: A.
- 2 Traverse the left subtree: PQR.
- 3 Traverse the right subtree: XYZ.

Apply these rules at each stage of the traversal.

- Begin at root . We get A.
- Move to the left subtree.

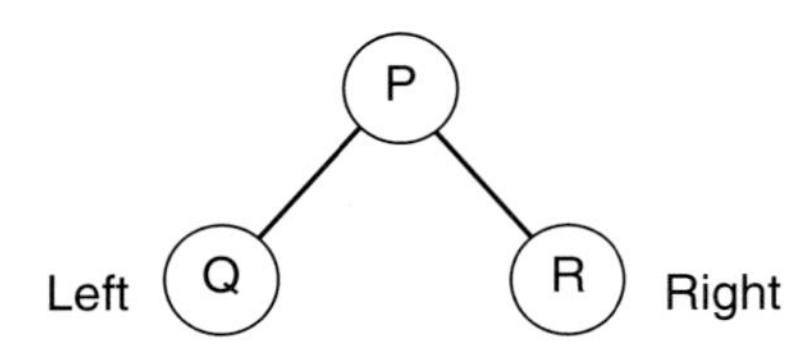

Since P is the root of this subtree, we now have AP.

- Move to the left of subtree, Q, then to the right of subtree, R. Since Q and R are leaf nodes, we can apply the preorder rules in full.

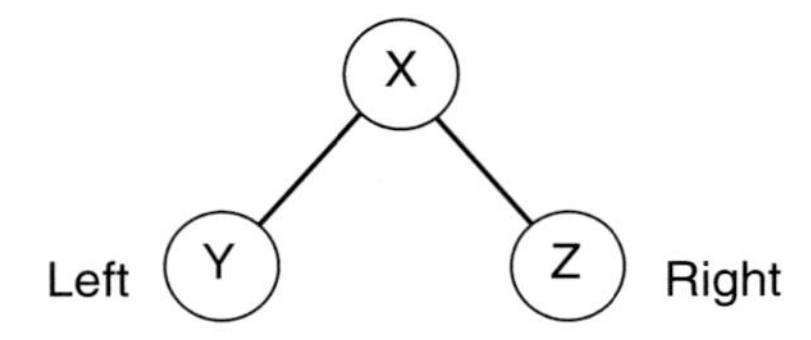

So we have APQR.

- Move to the right subtree.
- Apply the preorder rules: root, left, right.

We get APQRXYZ.

Formal description for Inorder
- Traverse left subtree (call this recursively until leaf node).
- Print root node data.
- Traverse right subtree (call this recursively until leaf node).

Inorder
- 1 Traverse the left subtree.
- 2 Visit the root node.
- 3 Traverse the right subtree.

Start at the leftmost node, Q.

- At this point, apply the inorder rules given above: left, root, right.

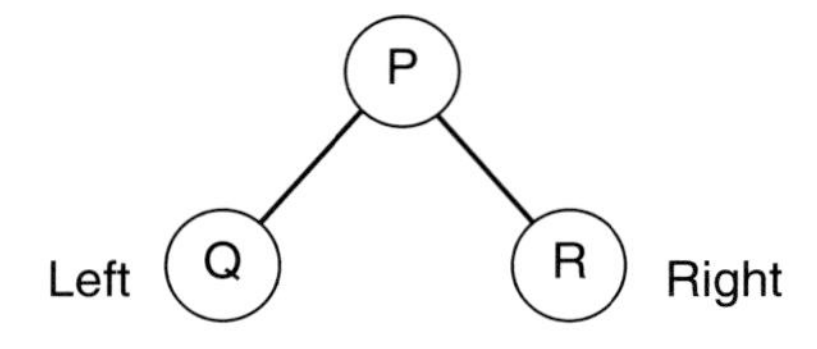

We get QPR.

Binary trees (continued)

- With the left subtree visited, now visit the root A. We have QPRA.
- Visit the right subtree.
- Apply the inorder rules: left, root, right.

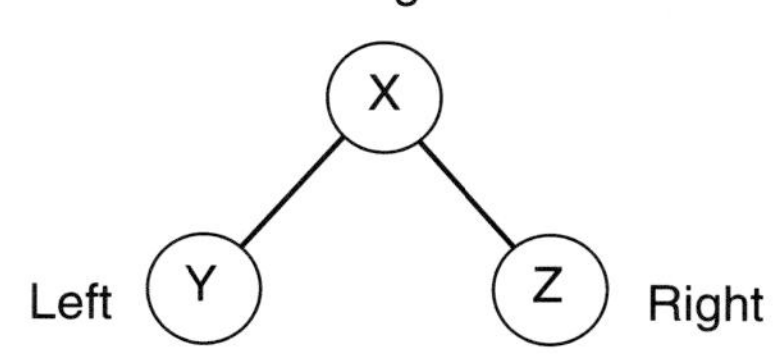

We get QPRAYXZ.

Formal description for Postorder
- Traverse left subtree (call this recursively until leaf node).
- Traverse right subtree (call this recursively until leaf node).
- Print root node data.

Postorder
This is also known as the Reverse Polish Notation.
- 1 Traverse the left subtree.
- 2 Traverse the right subtree.
- 3 Finish with the root node.

Start at the leftmost node, Q.

- At this point, apply the postorder rules: left, right, root.

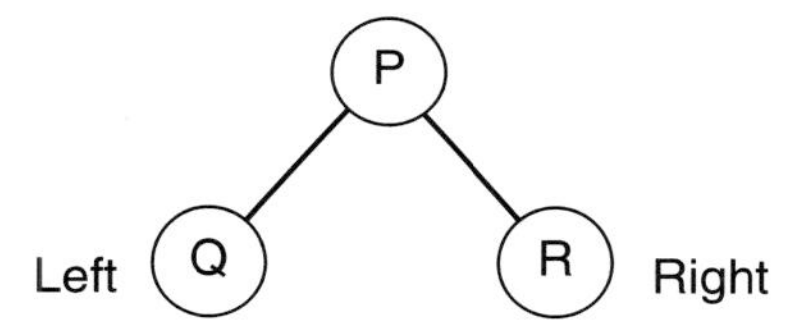

We get QRP.

- With the left subtree visited, now visit the right subtree.
- Apply the postorder rules: left, right, root.

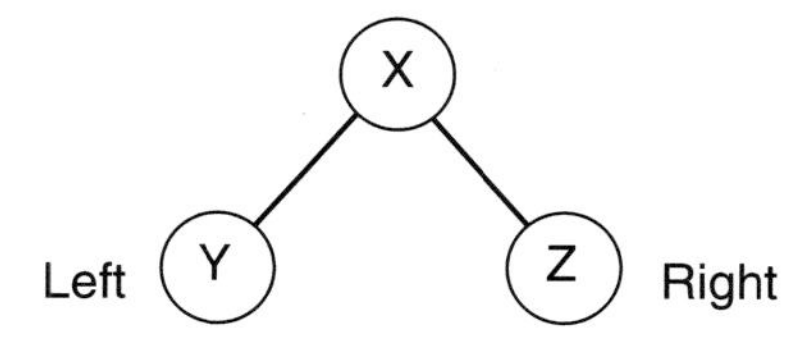

We get QRPYZX

- Now with the left and right subtrees visited, return to the root node.

We get QRPYZXA.

Static and dynamic data structures

Static data structures are used to good effect when an amount of memory needs to be set aside or reserved in order to store, manage or manipulate the required data.

An **array** is a static data structure which is defined within the program, its size is fixed and the required amount of memory is reserved. For example, if ten numbers were needed to be stored in memory, then:

In BASIC	**In Pascal**
DIM number (10)	Var number : array (1 . . . 10) of integer

These commands would reserve ten spaces for the numbers: that is, a one-dimensional array (a column of values). Below is an example of a one-dimensional array.

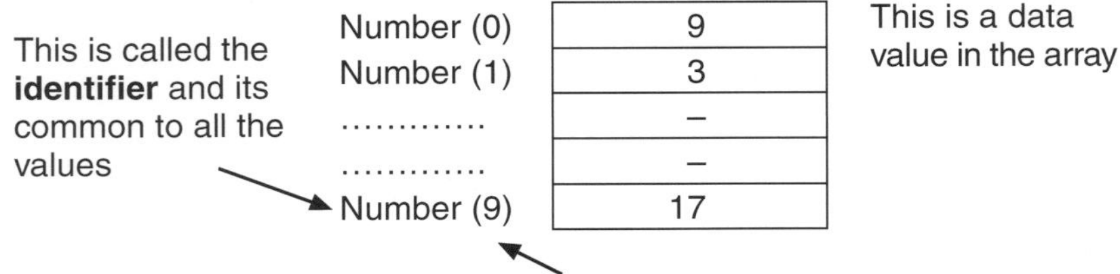

This is a subscripted variable and is used to uniquely identify each of the ten memory locations. Notice that the computer recognises 0 as the starting point rather than 1.

Note: This is the author's logical view of an array because it is easy to represent. However, by convention a one-dimensional array would be represented by a row rather than a column.

Sometimes, two-dimensional arrays are required when a table (rows and columns) is needed. For example: monthly statistical figures for five different shops.

In BASIC DIM stats (12,5)
In Pascal Var stats : array [1 . . . 12, 1 . . . 5] of real

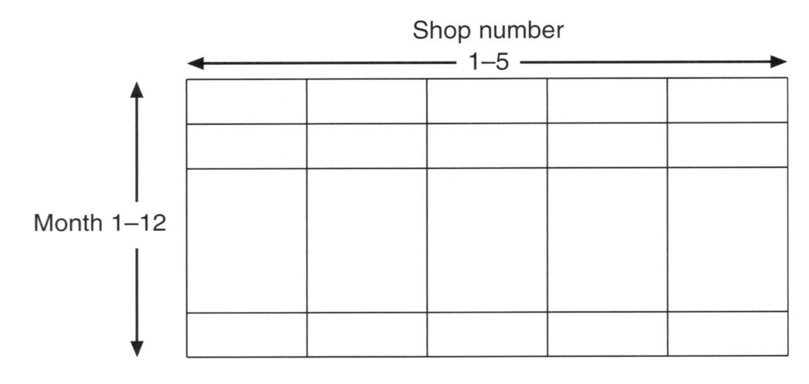

So, stats (3, 4) would refer to the statistics for the third month and shop number 4.

Records

Records can be arranged so that each field is of a fixed length and an array is used to store a maximum number of records. However, it must be noted that the record data structure is more versatile than the array in that each field could contain a different data type (for example, char, real, int, string) and that each field could be of variable length, thus making the structure dynamic. That is, the size of the structure may change during the execution of a program.

Files

Files are dynamic data structures in that they are not restricted in size by the program. The number of records can be added or deleted as necessary. However, a limiting factor on file size is usually governed by the amount of memory available (this is usually linked to the space on a disc).

Pointers

Pointer data types are used to good effect with linked lists, trees and queues, and help to create the dynamic nature of such data structures. When a new pointer is needed, it is taken from a reservoir of memory locations held in main memory, called the **heap**.

Data types	**Data structures**
• Character	• Lists
• Int	• Stacks
• Floating point	• Trees
• Boolean	• Arrays
• Real	• Queues
• Pointer	

Linked lists

A **linked list** is a dynamic data structure which incorporates items of data and a pointer system to link them together. The item could be an individual piece of data or it could even be a record of information treated as a unit. This unit is often called a node or a cell.

In a linked list, a pointer is needed to point to the start of the list. This is sometimes referred to as the **start pointer**. It basically gives the address in memory of the first data item.

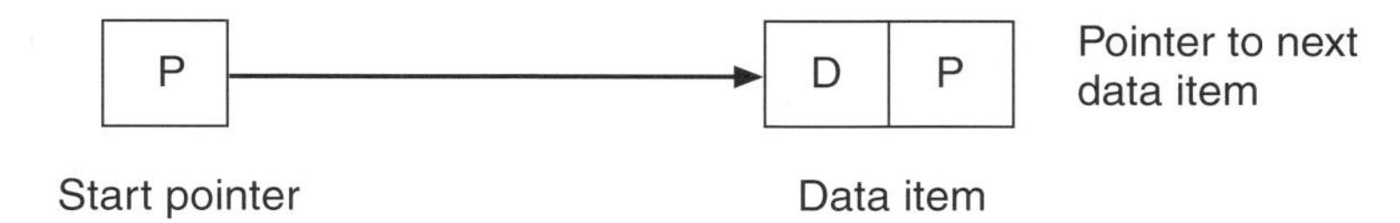

Let's use the following list to show how data and pointers are used.

Name (1) Ewan, Name (2) Joe, Name (3) Catherine, Name (4) Sameer, Name (5) Ben

If we wanted to represent the above list in alphabetical order, we could create a table with associated pointers.

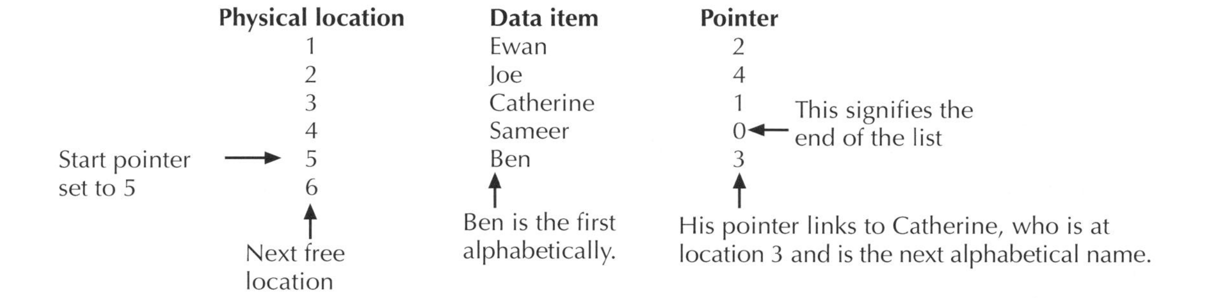

Physical location	Data item	Pointer
1	Ewan	2
2	Joe	4
3	Catherine	1
4	Sameer	0
5	Ben	3
6		

Start pointer set to 5 → 5

This signifies the end of the list (pointer 0)

Next free location (6)

Ben is the first alphabetically.

His pointer links to Catherine, who is at location 3 and is the next alphabetical name.

The above table would represent:

	Ben	First
	Catherine	Second
	Ewan	Third
	Joe	Fourth
and	Sameer	Fifth

Adding, deleting, searching and threading

Adding

To add the name Mark to the list and place it in its alphabetical position, we would do the following:

- Store Mark in the next free storage location: Name 6 in this case.
- Set the next free location to 7.
- Establish the position (alphabetically) where Mark is to be linked to.
- Alter the pointers before and after as necessary.

The table is now as follows:

Physical location	Data item	Pointer
1	Ewan	2
2	Joe	6 ← Now linked to Mark at location 6.
3	Catherine	1
4	Sameer	0
5	Ben	3
6	Mark	4
7		

Start pointer set to 5 → 5

New item added in the free location. His pointer links to Sameer at location 4.

With minor alterations to the table, a new value is added and the pointers adjusted accordingly.

Linked lists (continued)

Deleting

To delete the name Joe from the above list, we simply need to adjust the pointers. We would do the following:

- The name before Joe alphabetically, Ewan, has to have the pointer redirected to the next name alphabetically, which is Mark at location 6.
- The next free location is now location 2. That is, the location which Joe once occupied.

The table is now as follows:

	Physical location	Data item	Pointer
	1	Ewan	6
	2		
	3	Catherine	1
	4	Sameer	0
Start pointer set to 5 →	5	Ben	3
	6	Mark	4

The next free location is now 2.

Note Continuously inserting and deleting can become quite involved and require careful monitoring of free memory.

Searching

To search for a specific record or a particular name, we simply set the data item to the name to be found: for example, Data = Ewan.

The program will search either until it finds the name, in which case it will report 'Found', or until the search fails, in which case it will report 'Not found'.

Threading

This involves tracing (threading) a link from the start pointer, through the list, following the pointers until the end of the list.

File concepts

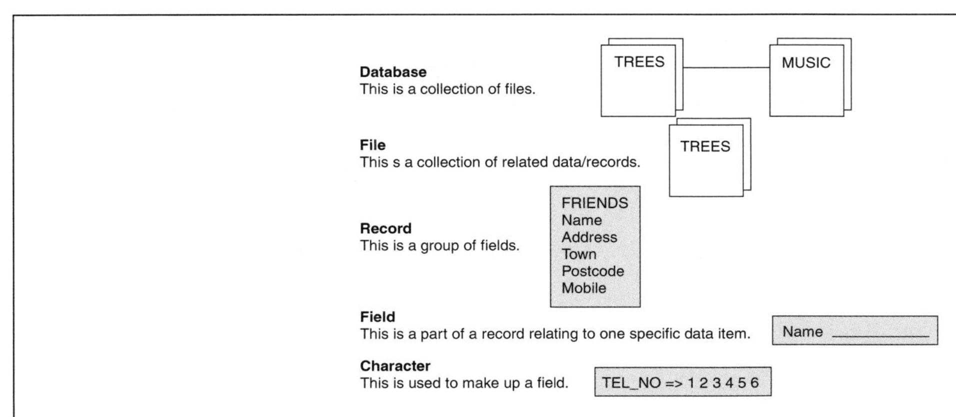

Key fields

Each record in a file should have a field that is *unique* to help to identify it from all the others. Fields such as National Insurance Number, Medical Number, ID number, are often used. This unique key field is called the **primary key**.

Sometimes, it is useful to identify a **group** of records in a file: for example, comedy videos, departments in a school, orders over £5000. These non-unique fields are referred to as **secondary keys**.

It is sometimes necessary to use several fields together to identify a specific record. This type of key field is called a **composite key field**. For example, in a supermarket, aisle number and shelf number could be used to locate a product. This is similar to a row and a column being used to identify a cell in a spreadsheet.

Fixed and variable length records

Fixed	Variable
• During design the record length is decided • The length is the same for each record in the file • Usually calculated in bytes or characters • Easily processed • Can be wasteful of space	• The record length is determined by the amount of data needed • Useful for free text • Saves space • Records more compact in the file • Processing is more complex • Needs end of field and/or end of record markers • Difficult to estimate the eventual file size

File types and extensions

Text files	Non-text files
• Sometimes called ASCII files • Used to transfer textual data between programs • This is a file type which is acceptable to most computers • The most common means of transferring data between application packages	• Special characters are used to preserve the formatting of a document. • Used to transfer tabular data between applications • Can be used to store pictures, source and object code, etc

Sometimes a **file name extension** is added to the file name in order to identify the specific file type. For example, Microsoft uses the following extensions to identify particular packages.

Word processing	Word	.doc	Presentation	Powerpoint	.ppt
Spreadsheet	Excel	.xls	Database	Access	.mdb

Master file	Transaction file	Reference file
• This is the main file • It contains data which is mostly permanent • It is usually updated with transient data from the transaction file	• Used to capture data which is not static: for example, sales this week, books borrowed this month • Used to update the master file • Usually sorted into the same order as the master file for easy updating	• This file contains data which does not change very often • It is used for look-up purposes, such as prices of goods, lists of materials

File structure

This relates to the data which is going to be used in the file. It should be used wisely by the programmer to help find data items and process the data in a variety of ways.

Data types

Text Allows letters, numbers and special characters.
AutoNumber Numbers the fields in sequence.
Number Only allows numbers in the field.
Currency A special type of number field represented to two decimal places.
Yes/No Only allows Yes or No. Sometimes called Boolean.
Lookup wizard Enables the user to select from a set of options: for example, days of the week.
Date / Time Restricts the input to a date or a time.

The following table shows a typical set of data items used for a file relating to customers.

Customer file

Field name	Example	Data type	Field length
Customer number	0001	AutoNumber	4
Customer name	Bloggs	Text	20
Address	23 Key Road	Text	20
Town	London	Text	20
Postcode	WC2 4XP	Text	8
Invoice date	03/09/01	Date / Time	8
Payment	Y	Boolean	1
Amount	£2000.37	Currency	8
Receipt	Y	Boolean	1
			90 **Total**

File size

Calculating the file size can be important, as it can determine the medium used for storage and data transfer.

When the records are the same size:

File size = Number of records × Record size

In the example above, each record has 90 characters or 90 bytes, since 1 byte stores one character.

A block size is typically 512 bytes. So each block could hold five records of 90 bytes (90 × 5=450) with some space left over. The file size would be calculated as follows.

Suppose, for example, we have 100 records, then:

$$\frac{\text{Number of records}}{\text{Number of records per block}} = \frac{100}{5} = 20 \text{ blocks}$$

Number of blocks at $\frac{1}{2}$k $= 20 \times \frac{1}{2} = 10$k (1k = 1024 bytes, so $\frac{1}{2}$k = 512 bytes.)

Hence, file size = 10k

Note A few bytes are usually taken up in each block for processing data: that is, end of record markers, record size, for example.

Physical record	Logical record
• This refers to the block of information to be written to or read. • A block usually contains several records • A hardware feature	• This refers to the organisation of the data in terms of files, records and fields • A software feature

Note The **blocking factor** is the number of logical records in each physical record.

File access and organisation

When file organisation is being considered, an essential feature is the number of records likely to be processed at any given time. This activity is referred to as the **hit rate**. It measures the number of records to be processed divided by the total number of records in the file and is expressed as a percentage value.

Serial files

- Medium is tape.
- Items of data are read, one at a time, in the order in which they are stored.
- No particular order.
- Items of data may vary in length provided there is a marker to signify starts and ends.

Serial file updates

Adding new records Go to the end of the file and add the new data.

Deleting records A new file needs to be created where only the records that are required are copied over and the unwanted records are therefore deleted. The original tape can then be overwritten.

Editing records To change data on a record requires a new copy of that record to be made. This may require the record to be deleted (as above), taking care to keep a copy of the record information, then add the amended record (as above).

Sequential files

- Medium is tape or disc.
- Items of data are read, one at a time, in key order.
- The items of data are ordered into a particular sequence: for example, alphabetical.
- Ideal for batch systems where the whole file has to be processed.
- Ideal when the hit rate is high.

Sequential file updates

Adding new records Since the records are in a predetermined order, adding a new record requires a new file to be created with the existing records copied up to the position of the new record, the new record added, then the remainder of the records copied.

Deleting records Copying all the records except the unwanted ones creates a new file.

Editing records Method is the same as for serial access.

Index sequential

- Medium is disc.
- An index is used to locate a starting position from where a sequential search takes place.
- Both the file and the index must be in some predetermined sequence.

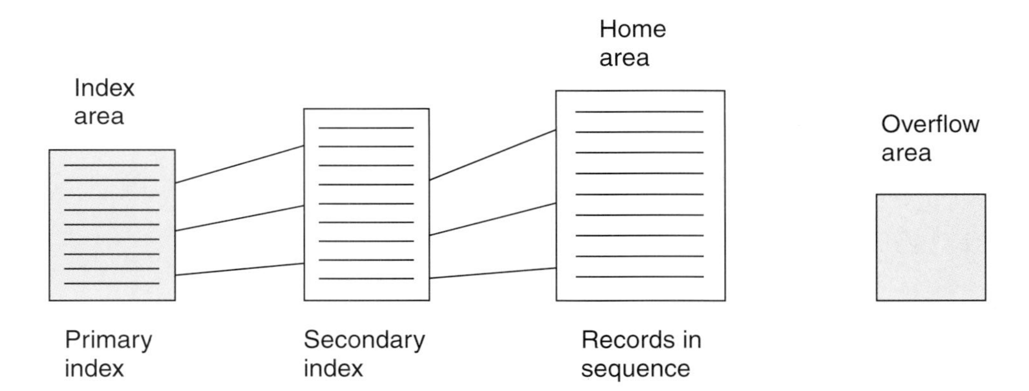

- This method usually allows for some space in the home area for additions and deletions without losing efficiency.
- An overflow area is often used for new (added) records which cannot fit into the home area. However, when this becomes very large, a special file-maintenance program is run to create a new file, putting all records in sequence again.
- This system only becomes inefficient when too many records are out of order due to numerous additions and deletions.

File access and organisation (continued)

Index sequential updates

Adding new records The key field of the new record is examined to ascertain its logical position in the file. The index, which places the pointer closest to the correct insert position, is selected. A sequential search begins from the selected index position to place the new record correctly. If there is insufficient space in the home area, the record is placed in the overflow area.

Deleting records The key field of the record to be deleted is examined to ascertain its logical position in the file. The index, which places the pointer closest to the required record, is selected. A sequential search begins from the selected index position to find the required record. The record is flagged as deleted but not actually deleted.

Editing records The record to be edited is selected as with deleting records above. The record is edited as required. The new record is used to overwrite the existing one in the same logical position.

Direct files

- Medium is disc.
- Any item can be retrieved immediately by generating its required address on the disc.
- A hashing or normalisation algorithm (mathematical formula) is used to generate the address where the record is to be stored. It does this by using the record key (account number, for example), and applying the formula to it.
- When the same addresses are generated for different keys, a 'collision' occurs. In this case, the next free address is often used to store the data and a flag used to point to the new location.
- Ideal for low hit rate activity.

Hashing algorithms should allow records to be added, deleted and updated in the most efficient way. They should also keep the number of collisions as low as possible.

Random (direct) file updates

Adding new records The key field of the new record is examined to ascertain its address. The address is calculated by applying the hashing function to the key. If the address is occupied, the record is placed in the next free space, otherwise it is placed at the calculated address.

Deleting records The key field of the record to be deleted is used by the hashing function to find the required address. Once found, the record is flagged as deleted. The record is still physically on the file but logically deleted. This allows the address to be used for forward addressing in the case of collisions.

Note that addresses are Occupied, Vacant or Flagged.

Editing records The record to be edited is found by applying the hashing function to its key. The record is edited as required. The new record is used to overwrite the existing one in the same logical position.

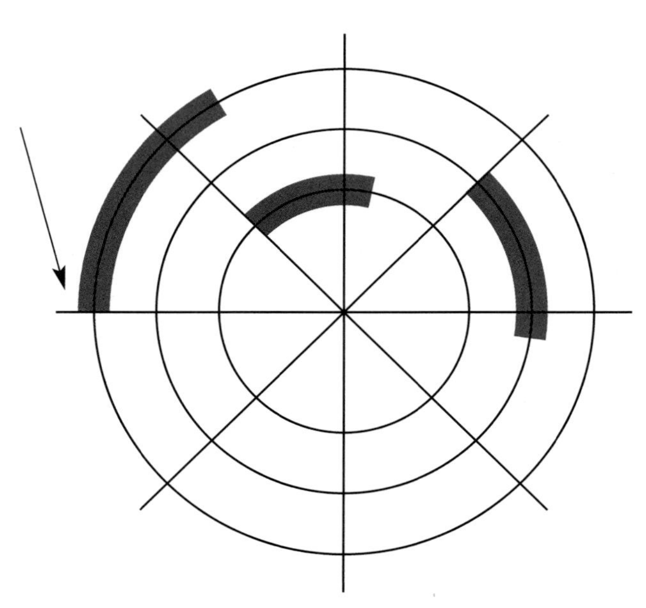

File operations

Creation	A new file is designed in terms of its structure and purpose
Reading	This is the process of taking a copy of the data from a file
Searching	There are various methods of searching for a record depending on the type of file organisation being used
Merging	Two or more files are merged by interweaving their records to form one file which still has its records in order
Updating	This involves altering existing data that has been written to the file. It could consist of adding new records or deleting old ones
Sorting	This means to sort data in a file into some predetermined order.
Appending	This is adding new data at the end of existing data

Updating methods

1 When using serial or sequential organised files, updating is usually done by copying. For example, a master file is updated by copying the data from a transaction file onto it. When copies are kept of the original files, these are called **generations**. This procedure is known as the Grandfather, Father, Son principle because usually three generations are kept before discarding the originals.

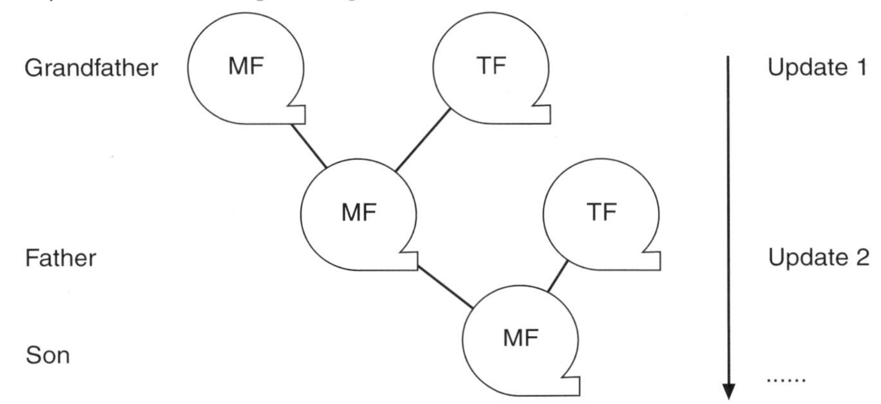

2 When using indexed sequential or direct access file organisation, the update procedure is usually by **overlay**. Since the required data can be specifically accessed, this data can be read into memory, altered as required and finally written back to its original address position.

3 File maintenance is an essential feature of any data processing environment. Its purpose is to ensure that the files are in their most accurate, useful, up-to-date and efficient state. Regular updating is a key feature of maintenance.

Merging two files using tape

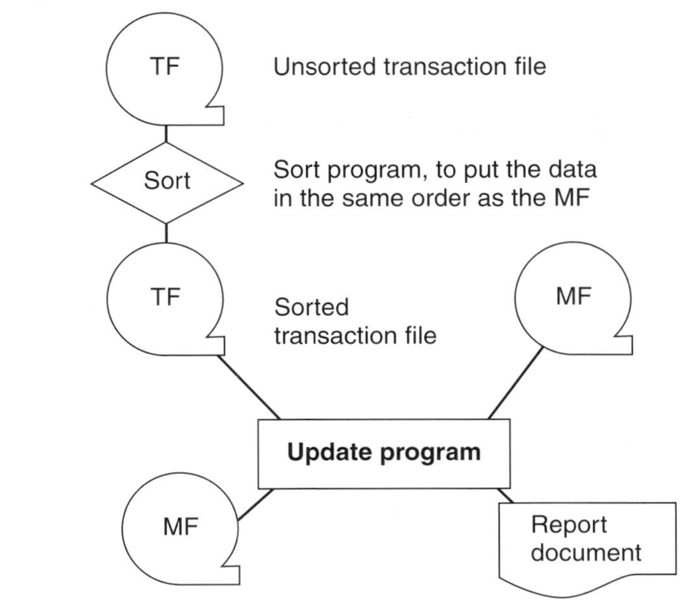

File security

Keeping data safe is of paramount importance. Large organisations spend vast sums of money in their endeavour to protect data from accidental or deliberate loss or damage.

Possible dangers to data

Accidental	Deliberate
• Natural hazards such as fire and flood • Hardware failure • Software malfunction • Unintentionally overwritten • Updated with incorrect data	• Fraud • Hacking: illegal access to data • Terrorism • Malicious tampering

Safeguards

Physical safeguards
- Restricting access to certain areas of a building or organisation.
- Security cameras.
- Alarm system.
- Lockable doors and windows.
- Keep important files in a fireproof safe.
- Keep replica copies of files in another building in case of major acts of terrorism or natural disaster.
- Use passes to regulate access to different areas.

Software safeguards
- User IDs and passwords are used to prevent unauthorised users from gaining access to the system.
- Restricted access rights prevent entry to certain areas of the system.
- Read only data ensures that it cannot be changed.
- A transaction log is used to monitor the system in terms of when a user logged on, what files were accessed and when the user logged off.

System failure safeguards
- Back-ups of files are made and stored in a safe place. This could mean dumping files periodically onto disc or tape to facilitate recovery, or keeping several generations of a file.

Data encryption
This is used to provide security to data both when stored electronically and when being transmitted over a network. An encoding and decoding algorithm is used to mix up the data so that unauthorised users cannot easily read it.

Data integrity

This refers to the correctness of the data. When data has not been adversely altered or corrupted, it is said to have **integrity**.

Errors must be detected as easily as possible to minimise the time and effort needed to rectify their adverse effect. A number of validation techniques can be used.

Character type check	The type of data to be expected might be numbers only, letters only
Field length check	The field has a maximum number of characters: for example, date has eight characters – DD/MM/YY
Range check	The number entered must be within a certain range: for example, 1 to 100
Check digit	A number appended to a code for self checking: for example, modulus 11
Presence check	Ensures a field is not left blank
Hash total	This is where a set of numerical values are added together to give the hash total. Usually, a meaningless total used solely for checking purposes
Batch total	This could represent the number of documents, items or records in a batch
Control total	This total is formed by adding the value of a numeric field in each record. It acts as a double check when the batch items are being entered

Verification
This is a manual check.

- It can be carried out by pre-input checks: namely, reading over the information on source documents to make sure that all the necessary data has been given.
- It can sometimes involve two operators keying in the same document and allowing the computer to verify the accuracy of the data entry by highlighting any mismatches.

Database systems

A **database** is a collection of data that is centrally organised and is structured so that it can be accessed by a number of different applications. It is sometimes thought of as a collection of files but this view can trivialise the concept somewhat, especially if the files are unrelated.

In a database system, the various departments in an organisation can enter the data and it can then be accessed by all the other applications. So, for example, the sales department, marketing department and stock control department can contribute to and access the same pool of data.

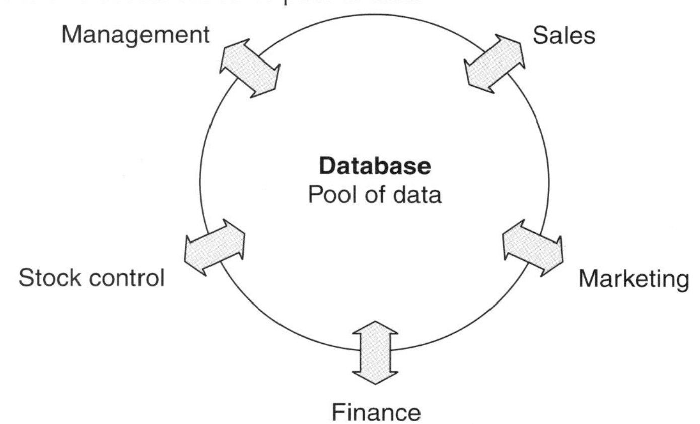

Even with the most careful planning of the record structures, there are occasions when alterations have to be made: for example, a field has to be added or deleted. This will involve making changes to all the applications programs so that consistency is preserved. In a fixed length record structure, it is essential that every record is the same size even if the data content is radically different.

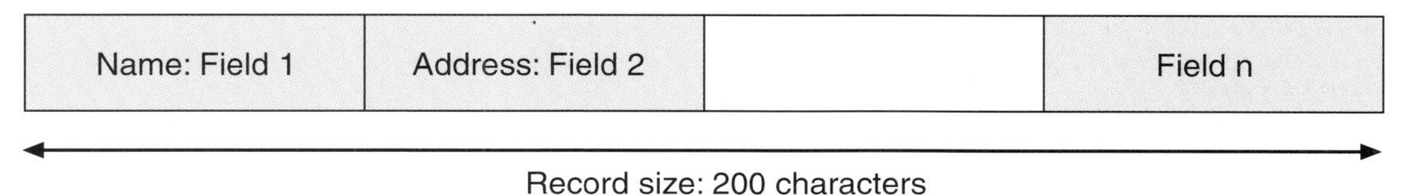

The record size (structure) must be consistent. Therefore, all the programs have to be altered to preserve this. This makes the programs dependent on the record size.

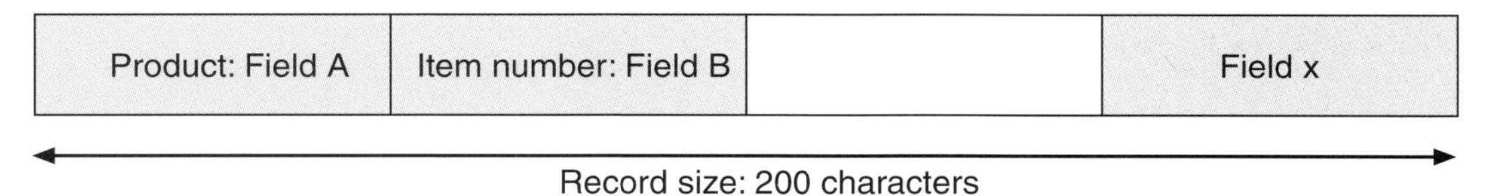

Data which is stored in one large file is called a **flat file**. More often than not, a database contains a collection of files which are shared between a variety of applications. Preserving the integrity and security of the data is important but this can be difficult to maintain due to the common pool of data being accessible to every application or user.

Multi-user database systems

It is likely that the data in a database will be drawn from a number of different sources and will therefore be used for more than one purpose and by more than one person or department. In a multi-access environment, the database software enables more than one person to be able to read or update data from the same tables concurrently. This apparent freedom can create potential problems if not monitored or supervised properly.

Problems	Solutions
• Locking all data. Users can only read the data. They cannot update it • Several users attempting to update a record at the same time • Data seems to be constantly locked	• Give appropriate access rights to individuals or groups of users, thus restricting what can be done • The first user request has the record for them, thus restricting the update to a single user • After a fixed period of time, the data is available on general release: that is, unlocked therefore avoiding potential deadlock

Database management system (DBMS)

A **database management system** is a complex software system that is used to create, develop and maintain the database. Due to the dynamic nature of a database, certain functions need to be carried out:

- An interface established with the user program.
- Storage requirements met for all the data and programs.
- Updates to the data efficiently carried out.
- Security of data strictly controlled.
- Back-up and recovery of data available.
- Data consistency preserved.
- Data duplication / redundancies controlled.
- Data independence: that is, the programs which access the database are not dependent on the structure of the data.

Database administrator (DBA)

The **database administrator** is the person who is in charge of the database. He/she needs to have an extensive knowledge of the organisation and its data requirements. The DBA has overall control of the database and would be a very powerful figure in the organisation. The duties of the DBA would include:

- Design and set up the database.
- Maintaining the database.
- Alter the structure as the business needs change.
- Set passwords for user access levels.
- Training for the users of the database.
- Maintaining a data dictionary.
- Ensuring that the system runs as efficiently as possible.
- Maintaining the security of the database.

The schema

The database can be viewed or perceived from a number of different levels. The entire database view is referred to as a **schema** and the different views are called the **subschema**. There are three main levels.

First level : conceptual level (schema)

This refers to the view that the design team have of the database. Together they represent a combined view of the entire database. The design of the conceptual schema is the responsibility of the DBA and his / her team.

Second level : external level (schema)

This refers to the view of the database by individual users. The database will be used by a variety of different departments and users with different needs within a department. Therefore, the perception of what the database can deliver will vary.

The DBA sets the access level which controls where each user can gain access to the third level. He/she does this by setting the read/write privileges.

Third level : internal (storage) level (schema)

This describes how the data will be stored on the actual storage medium. The file details, access method and organisation are viewed at this level, if not physically at least logically.

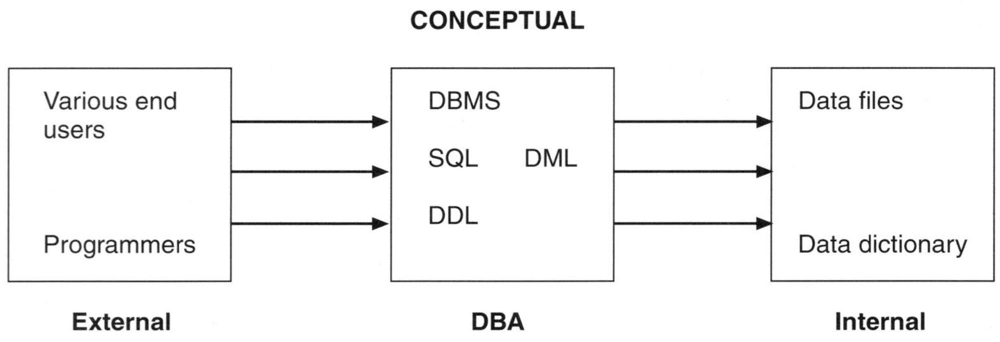

CONCEPTUAL

Various end users
Programmers

DBMS
SQL DML
DDL

Data files
Data dictionary

External **DBA** **Internal**

Data dictionary

The **data dictionary** contains information about the actual database itself. This data enables the DBA to keep a tight control over all aspects of the database and facilitates maintenance. The dictionary could contain:

- A detailed description of each data item.
- The relationships between data items.
- Access rights for users and groups.
- Validation rules.
- The map between the logical and the physical view for storage purposes.
- Data recovery procedures.
- A transaction log to monitor the users, programs and data.

Database languages

DDL – Data description language
The DBA would use this special language to help with the database model. The DDL is used to define the entities and their attributes (see page 72). The logical structure of the database is defined in terms of files, records and fields and their interrelationship within the system. This is sometimes called the **data definition language**.

DML – Data manipulation language
This language enables the DBA to make any alterations to the database. It has built-in features which can be used to modify the data in a variety of different ways. The query features enable all users to manipulate the data within the restricted zone to which they have been given access by the DBA.

SQL – Structured query language
The query language provides the end users with the opportunity to interrogate the database. Queries can be drawn from a combination of tables and can be complex in nature. A variety of options are available with each query, such as being able to select specific fields, set criteria, sort the data and hide fields.

SQL can be used to great effect to extract the information contained in the database. Although SQL can be used for other functions, its primary objective is to facilitate the user in querying the database.
Some of the constructs used with SQL are:

SELECT — This identifies the fields which are to be considered for the query.

FROM — Identifies the table from which the data is to be taken.

WHERE — This can be used with conditions. For example: SELECT age FROM tbl.student WHERE age > "14". Here, tbl. stands for table.

ORDER BY — This enables the user to specify the way the data is displayed (for example, ascending / descending order) on a specific field.

GROUP BY — This provides the facility of selecting specific data items and grouping them together so that further processing can be carried out on the group.

Data can also be queried by example (QBE). This is used in MS Access. With this method the user can:

- Select data from two or more related tables.
- Select which fields are to be used from the chosen tables.
- Sort the data on a specific field.
- Enter criteria on which a search is performed: for example, Age > 21.
- Save the query for future use.

The results of this query are stored in a new table and saved with a user defined name.

Data modelling

When large databases are being designed, it has become common practice to use diagrams. These are often referred to as **data models**. Each model has a number of key elements.

Entities These refer to the people, places or things represented in the database: for example, cities, students, stock.

Attributes These refer to the information or facts relating to the entity: for example, City – name, Student – number.

In order to link these features of the data model, a relationship has to be created.

Relationships These provide the links between the entities. For example:

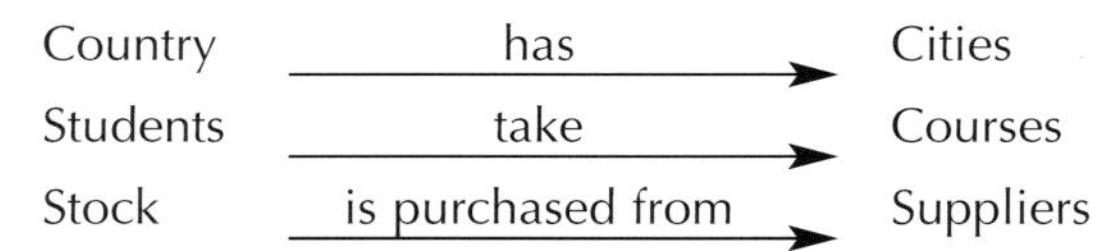

Entity relationship diagrams (ER diagrams)

These diagrams are graphical representations of the structure of data. ER diagrams allow the analyst to think about and model general relationships. There are four possible relationships linking the entities.

One-to-one relationship

Country 1 —— has ——> 1 Capital City

Each country has one capital city.

One-to-many relationships

Customer 1 —— places ——> *m* Orders

A customer can place many orders.

Many-to-one relationship

Patients *m* —— occupy ——> 1 Ward

Many patients can occupy a ward.

Many-to-many relationship

Students *m* —— study ——> *m* Courses.

Many students study many courses.

Database models

There are three main models used for databases.

Hierarchical model

This is where data is held in a tree structure and is used mainly with mini and mainframe systems.

Network model

Data can be retrieved very quickly from the database, making this model particularly suited to applications where specific requests are made on a regular basis. It is mainly used with mini- and mainframe systems.

Relational model

This has become the most widely used model for microcomputer systems. The data is held in a collection of tables that are linked together using relationships.

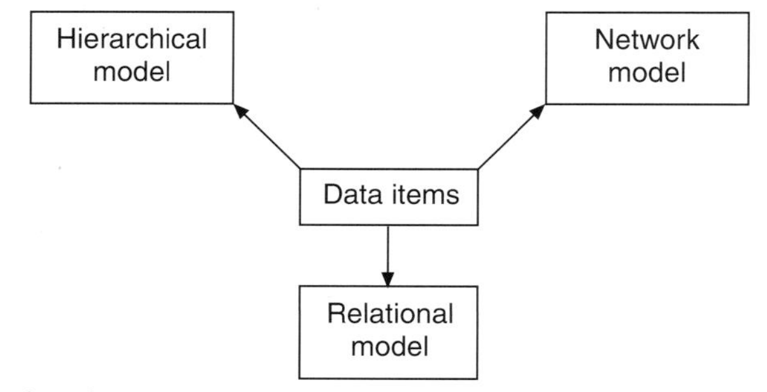

The data is organised, managed and manipulated using a particular database model.

Relational database

A single file held on a relational database is called a **flat file**. It provides a basic structuring of the data and is fairly simple to set up and use. For example: a record structure with ten fields A – J, giving a single table flat file.

A	B	C	D	E	F	G	H	I	J
–	–	–	–	–	–	–	–	–	–
–	–	–	–	–	–	–	–	–	–
–	–	–	–	–	–	–	–	–	–

A much more efficient method for representing the data is to create smaller tables which are linked together.

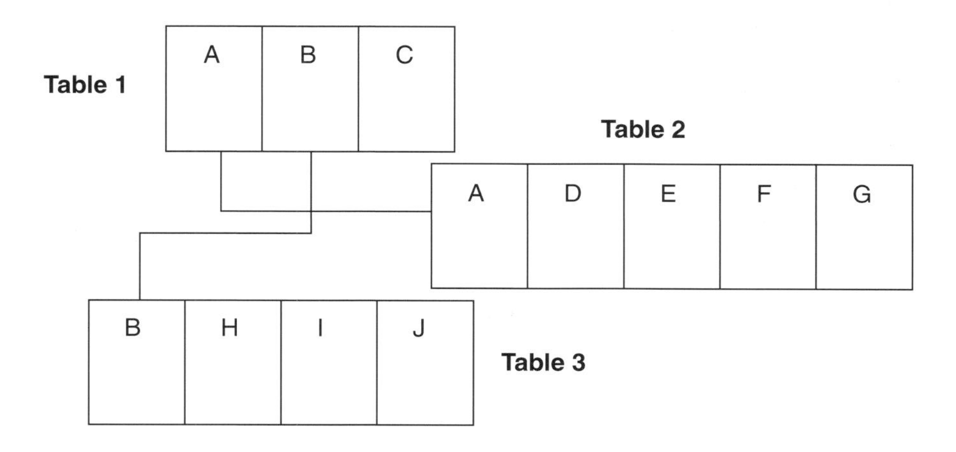

The process by which these tables are created is called **normalisation**.

Relational database notation
A table is basically a file and must be given a suitable name: for example, student, class. Table names are usually written in capitals and the attributes (fields) are enclosed in brackets: for example, TABLE – NAME (—).

Each table has a key which is used as a unique identifier. When the key is a single attribute, it is referred to as a **primary key**. However, the key can be made up from two or more attributes, in which case it is called a **composite key**.

The key is usually indicated within the brackets by being listed first and underlined. For example:

TABLE – NAME (<u>Primary key</u>, data items)
TABLE – NAME (<u>Composite key</u>, data items)

When a key from one table is used in another, this is called a **foreign key**. Foreign keys are used to link tables together. For example:

TABLE – NAME (<u>Primary key</u>, foreign key, data items)

Normalisation

When a database conforms to certain constraints, it is said to be normalised, or in **normal form**. Normalisation is a way of ensuring that the data is more efficiently represented and processed.

There are at least five normal forms (sets of rules) but only the first three are often used or needed. These still produce many automatic advantages. For example:

- The designer is forced to go into the data requirements of a particular organisation in detail.
- There is a minimum of data duplication: that is, little redundancy.
- There is protection against updates causing problems. That is, when data in one place is altered, added or deleted, the effects of that update are automatic
- There is a more efficient storage of the data.
- A relational database gives the organisation the ability to change as situations or legislation dictate. This flexibility is one of the biggest advantages.

The stages in normalization are:

First normal form (1NF) Remove repeating groups.

Second normal form (2NF) Ensure full functional dependency on the whole key.

Third normal form (3NF) Remove transitive dependencies.

Consider the following flat file and then normalise it using the three stages outlined above. The file refers to a business which sells nuts, bolts, screws and nails etc.

ORDER

Order #	**Customer #**	**Customer – Name**	**Customer – Address**
015769	0056	Mr R Parkinson	3 Bree Road
042561	0089	Mr T Patterson	17 Orange Park

Product #	**Product – Description**	**Quantity**	**Price**
756	Wire nails	100	£4.50
342	Oboe nails	50	£6.00
123	Brass screws	100	£5.25
756	Wire nails	50	£2.25
423	6″ bolts	5	£2.00

In standard notation:

ORDER (Order #, Customer #, Customer – Name, Customer – Address
(Product #, Product – Description, Quantity, Price))

From the table, it is clear to see that for each record Order #, Customer #, Customer – Name and Customer – Address are written once but Product #, Product – Description, Quantity and Price are repeated because several items have been selected.

Note In the standard notation, the inner bracket identifies the attributes that are repeated.

1NF
Remove repeating groups.

Primary key

ORDER (Order #, Customer #, Customer – Name, Customer – Address)

ORDER – LINE (Order #, Product #, Product – Description, Quantity, Price)

Composite key

Notice that Order # is used in both tables so that they can be linked together.

Normalisation (continued)

The tables are:

ORDER

Order #	Customer #	Customer – Name	Customer – Address
015769	0056	Mr R Parkinson	3 Bree Road
042561	0089	Mr T Patterson	17 Orange Park

ORDER – LINE

Order #	Product #	Product – Description	Quantity	Price
015769	756	Wire nails	100	£4.50
015769	342	Oboe nails	50	£6.00
042561	123	Brass screws	100	£5.25
042561	756	Wire nails	50	£2.25
042581	423	6″ bolts	5	£2.00

2NF

Ensure full functional dependency on the whole key.

The Order table is already in 2NF because it has a primary key and all the attributes are therefore dependent on the key.

However, ORDER – LINE has a composite key, which means that some of the attributes could be dependent on Order # alone or Product # alone but not both. In such cases, we have to remove the attributes and create another table.

Consider ORDER – LINE (Order #, Product #, Product – Description, Quantity, Price).

Order #, Product # —gives→ Quantity — We need the order number and the product number to get the quantity ordered.

Order #, Product # —gives→ Price — We need the order number and the product number to get the price of the goods ordered.

However,

Product # —gives→ Product – Description

Therefore, Product – Description is not dependent on the whole key but only a part of it. We have to remove it and create another table.

PRODUCT (<u>Product #</u>, Product – Description)

ORDER

Order #	Customer #	Customer – Name	Customer – Address
015769	0056	Mr R Parkinson	3 Bree Road
042561	0089	Mr T Patterson	17 Orange Park

ORDER – LINE

Order #	Product #	Quantity	Price
015769	756	100	£4.50
015769	342	50	£6.00
042561	123	100	£6,25
042561	423	5	£2.00

Normalisation (continued)

PRODUCT

Product	Product – Description
756	Wire nails
342	Oboe nails
123	Brass screws
423	6″ bolts

We now have the following three tables in 2NF:

ORDER (Order #, Customer #, Customer–Name, Customer–Address)
ORDER LINE (Order #, Product #, Quantity, Price)
PRODUCT (Product #, Product – Description)

In each entity, the non-identifying attributes are dependent on the key attribute.

3NF

Remove transitive dependencies. That is, is there a non-key attribute that it is not dependent on the key?

Consider each entity (table) to check for transitive dependencies and remove the dependencies between non-key attributes.

Primary key
PRODUCT (Product #, Product–Description)
Non-key attribute

Since there is only one non-key attribute, it must be in 3NF. That is, it cannot be dependent on another non-key attribute if there is none.

ORDER – LINE (Order #, Product #, Quantity, Price)
Composite key   Non-key attributes

The quantity does not give the price since the different products are priced differently, and the price does not give the quantity for the same reason as above. Therefore, ORDER LINE is in 3NF.

ORDER (Order #, Customer #, Customer – Name, Customer – Address).
Primary key   Non key attributes

Customer # would give the Customer – Name and it would give the Customer – Address. Therefore, this table is *not* in 3NF.

Remove the Customer – Name and Customer – Address with Customer # as the identifier to give:

CUSTOMER (Customer #, Customer – Name, Customer – Address)
ORDER (Order #, Customer #).

The four tables are:

ORDER

Order #	Customer #
015769	0056
042561	0089

PRODUCT

Product #	Product–Description
756	Wire nails
342	Oboe nails
123	Brass screws
423	6″ Bolts

Normalisation (continued)

ORDER – LINE

Order #	Product #	Quantity	Price
015769	756	100	£4.50
015769	342	50	£6.00
042561	123	100	£5.25
042561	756	50	£2.25
042561	423	5	£2.00

CUSTOMER

Customer #	Customer – Name	Customer – Address
0056	Mr R Parkinson	3 Bree Road
0089	Mr T Patterson	17 Orange Park

No transitive dependencies exist, so the four entities are in 3NF.

ORDER (Order #, Customer #)
CUSTOMER (Customer #, Customer – Name, Customer – Address)
ORDER – LINE (Order #, Product #, Quantity, Price)
PRODUCT (Product #, Product – Description)

Remember – ask: 'Does it rely upon the key? The whole key and nothing but the key?'

If the answer is 'Yes' to all three, then you have 3NF.

Note BCNF (Boyce, Codd Normal Form) is generally considered to be equivalent to 3NF.

Other database systems

Object oriented databases
In traditional database systems, the storage requirements have mainly been for files, records and fields. The data structure has been fairly easy to define and the data requirements mainly central. However, with the advent of multi-media and graphics-based applications, the data types have become more complex. In an object-oriented environment, data and its associated properties are stored as objects and these can be transmitted, stored and manipulated.

Open Database Connectivity (ODBC)
This type of system provides the means of accessing / sharing data created on one database (for example, Oracle or Paradox) with a different database program (for example, Access or SQL Server). The ODBC program enables the portability problems inherent in many software packages to be minimised. It can even allow the data in the database to be transmitted to other application software, thus providing a greater flexibility and communication potential.

Data transmission

Data communication is concerned with the sending and receiving of data from one device to another. There are many factors that affect transfer and this chapter will consider the main methods and features.

Serial transmission

Data is sent one bit after the other along a single data line. Although this may not appear to be the most efficient means of transferring data, very high rates are possible.

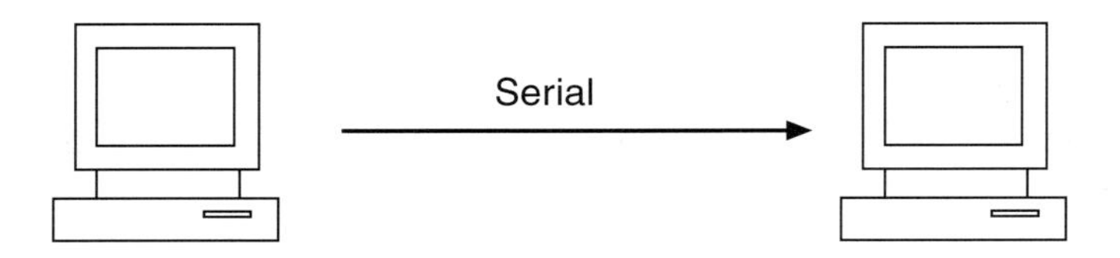

Note The **baud rate** is used to measure the speed of serial data transmission.

Parallel transmission

Data is sent along separate lines simultaneously. However, this method of transfer can only be used over short distances. The parallel port (interface) on a PC is often used for the printer since the cable is short.

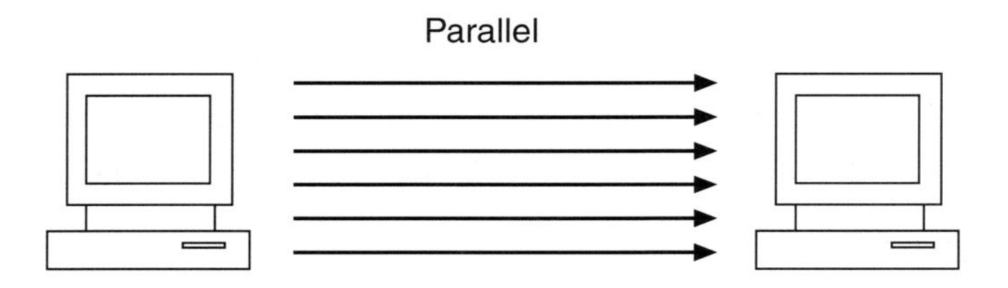

An SCSI port is a parallel port. This means the socket has many pins.

Bit rate

The speed at which data moves around the computer system is often referred to as the **bit rate**. This is measured in bits per second (bps). In the same way, character transfer can be measured in characters per second (cps).

Bandwidth

Data transmission speeds relate to signal frequencies. The rate at which a signal repeats itself every second is called its **frequency** and is measured in hertz. The range of frequencies which can be transmitted is known as the **bandwidth**. Therefore, the wider the bandwidth, the greater the volume of data that can be transmitted.

Synchronous and asynchronous data transmission

Asynchronous	Synchronous
• Sends one character at a time • Requires start and stop bits to be transmitted with each character • A parity bit is often sent as well to check for transmission errors.	• Data transfers are timed to coincide with the system clock pulses. • Blocks of characters may be transmitted synchronously. • High transfer rates are possible.

One data transfer at a time

Several data transfers at once

Data transmission (continued)

Parity

The parity system is used during data transmission to check that no errors have taken place. Odd parity systems check the number of 1s being sent and ensure that the total is always an odd number. For example:

10010010 There are two ones in this code along with a parity bit, which makes a total of three ones.

Parity bit set to 1 to ensure odd parity transfer is observed.

Handshaking

When signals are exchanged between devices in order to establish whether they are ready to send or receive data, this is known as **handshaking**.

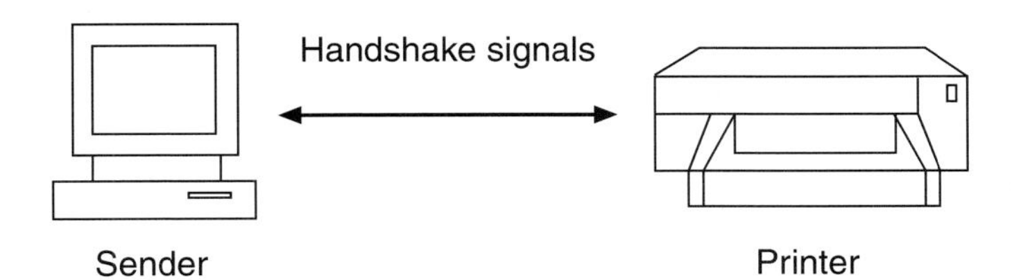

Transmission modes

Simplex → Data is transmitted in one direction only.

Half duplex ⇄ Data can be transmitted in both directions but only one at a time.

Duplex ↔ Data can be transmitted in both directions simultaneously.

Electronic data interchange (EDI)

- This enables users to exchange business documents, such as invoices and receipts, over the telephone network.
- Much quicker than conventional post and greatly reduces paperwork.
- Examples are:
  - Tradanet – which links manufacturers, wholesalers, distributors and retailers.
  - Brokernet – which links insurance companies and brokers.

Protocols

There are a strict set of rules which govern all aspects of computer operation. These rules are called **protocols**. Examples of data communication protocols are:

- **File transfer protocol (FTP)** This refers to the rules for transmitting data over a network.
- **Transmission control protocol/Internet protocol (TCP/IP)** This refers to the rules for data transfer between and within networks. It also includes data transfer across the Internet.

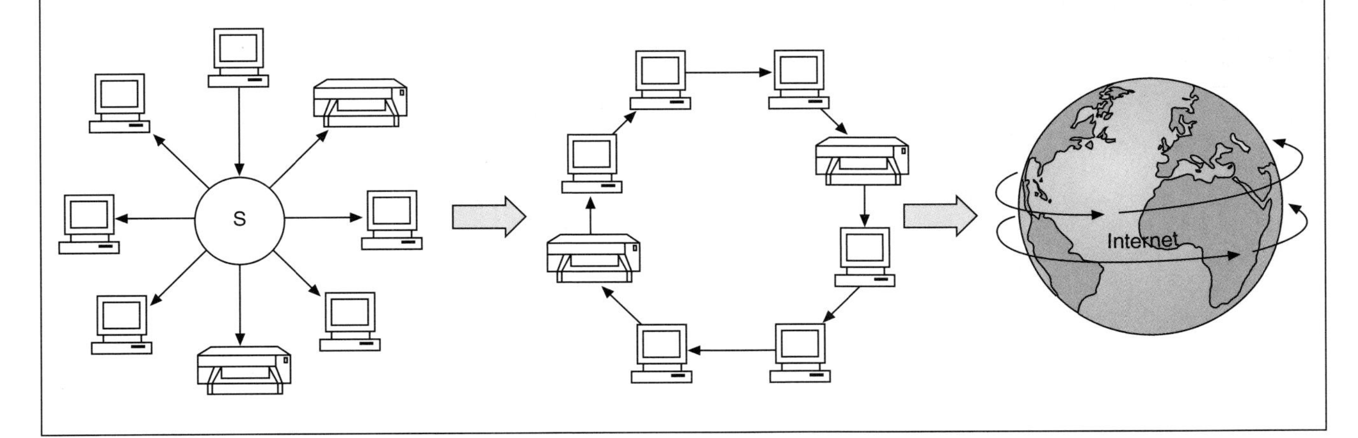

Communications media

Fibre optics cables
Light beams are used to carry the digital data. Data transmission is very fast, secure, virtually impossible to tap into, and not subject to electrical interference.

Coaxial cables
Data is transmitted at high speeds (used with TVs). The cable is well insulated. There are two types:

- **Baseband** This type carries one signal at a time, satisfactory over relatively short distances. Signals deteriorate over longer distances and need refreshing.
- **Broadband** This type can carry many signals on a carrier wave.

Twisted pair
This is a pair of copper wires twisted together with some insulation. Used effectively, they provide minimum interference to data. The great advantage is that the system is inexpensive.

Infrared communication
This is used to control remote devices. There needs to be a direct line between the transmitter and the receiver otherwise the infrared signal will be broken.

Microwave communication
The data moves along the wave in straight lines at high speed. Hence, the system needs line of sight between the transmitter and receiver.

Satellite communication
This is used for international communication. Large volumes of data are carried at high speed along narrow beams.

Integrated services digital network (ISDN)
This line requires a high bandwidth because it can carry a wide variety of data types, such as sounds, pictures, video computer data. Data is sent at high speed in a digital format, therefore no modems are needed as the whole operation is using digital data.

Modem

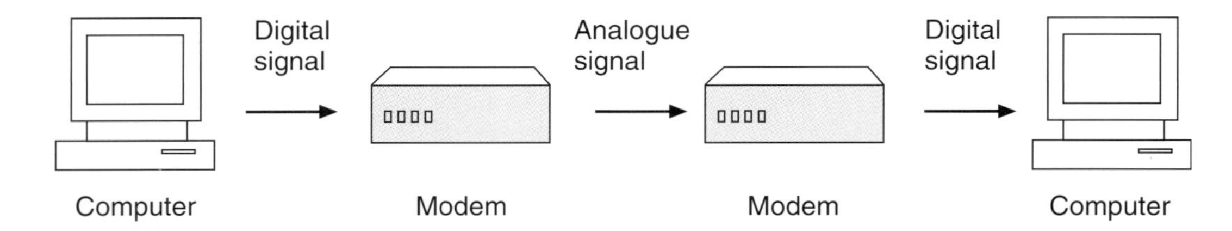

When data is sent via the conventional telephone line, the digital data must be converted into an analogue signal and then back into digital format by the modems at either end of the telephone line. This process of sending and receiving is carried out by the modems, **mo**dulating and then **dem**odulating the data.

(An analogue signal is a continuously varying signal. A digital signal has discrete intervals, being comprised of binary digits.)

Communication lines
The use of the communications infrastructure can be purchased in two main ways:

Public line use
This is called **dial-up networking**. Individuals and small businesses make most use of this facility. There is usually a fixed rental charge for the line plus a cost for use which depends on the distance required and the length of time the user is connected.

Private or leased lines
This is called **leased-line networking**. Large companies and organisations would make most use of this facility. There is a fixed annual fee and no further charge, and exclusive use of the line.

Asymmetric digital subscriber line (ADSL)
- This type of line caters for the transmission of video signals over ordinary telephone cables.
- There is a limit for ADSL of about 2.5 km (1.5 miles).
- Because of the digital connection, the transfer rates are faster than with the conventional modem and analogue system.

Networking

A computer that is not linked to other computers is referred to as a **stand-alone system**.

A **computer network** is a set of computers which are linked together and therefore capable of sharing a variety of resources, such as hardware, software and communication connections.

Advantages of networking

- Hardware resources, such as printers, scanners and communication devices, can be shared.
- Software resources, such as application programs, shared files and general purpose packages, are available to all users.
- Human resources, such as technical and administrative staff, can support the effective running of the organisation.
- Improved communication between users.
- Structural access to data and resources.

Disadvantages of networking

- The organisation can grind to a halt if the network goes down.
- The network can become very slow, especially at peak times.
- Keeping the system secure from internal and external negative influences.
- Mass disruption is possible if the network is not managed efficiently.

Wide area network (WAN)

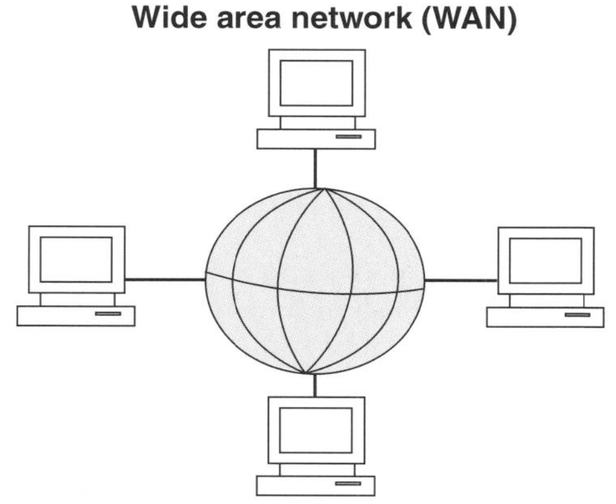

Computers are linked together over a wide geographical area.

Local area network (LAN)

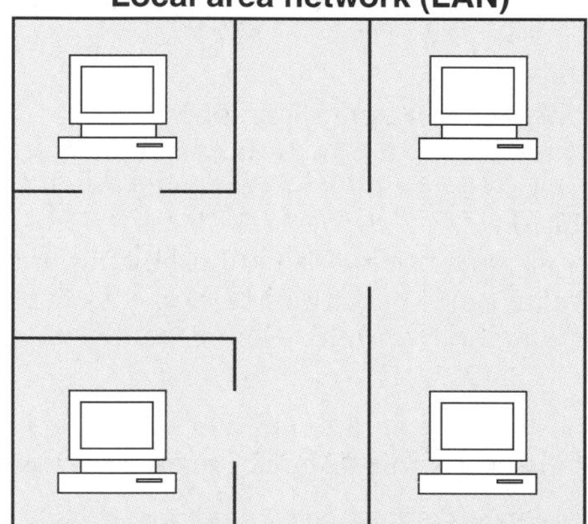

Computers are linked (quite often together in the same room or building) over a small geographical area.

Router	Gateway
• Used to connect two LANs together. Each LAN can be the same or of a different type (configuration) • A device used to redirect data packets to their eventual destination address	• These are used to link two networks together • They can alter the format of data packets to be transmitted on a LAN with a different protocol structure

Value added networks

- This is a wide area network with extra features provided at additional cost.
- BT provide WANs, such as Satstream, Megastream and Switchstream.
- Other facilities, such as e-mail, facsimile, reference databases and bulletin boards, can be added to existing network features.

Peer-to-peer networking	Server-based networking
• A small computer network with only a few terminals • Resources such as printers and storage are shared • All computers have equal status and have similar specifications • The computers function as stand-alone machines but have communication facilities • No special network OS is needed. • There is no dedicated file server or printer server	• A file server is used to provide a common service to all the computers on the network • Software is held at the server and shared as required • This is more expensive but provides added security, speed and power • Back-ups of files are taken regularly and controlled by the server

Network configurations

Linear bus

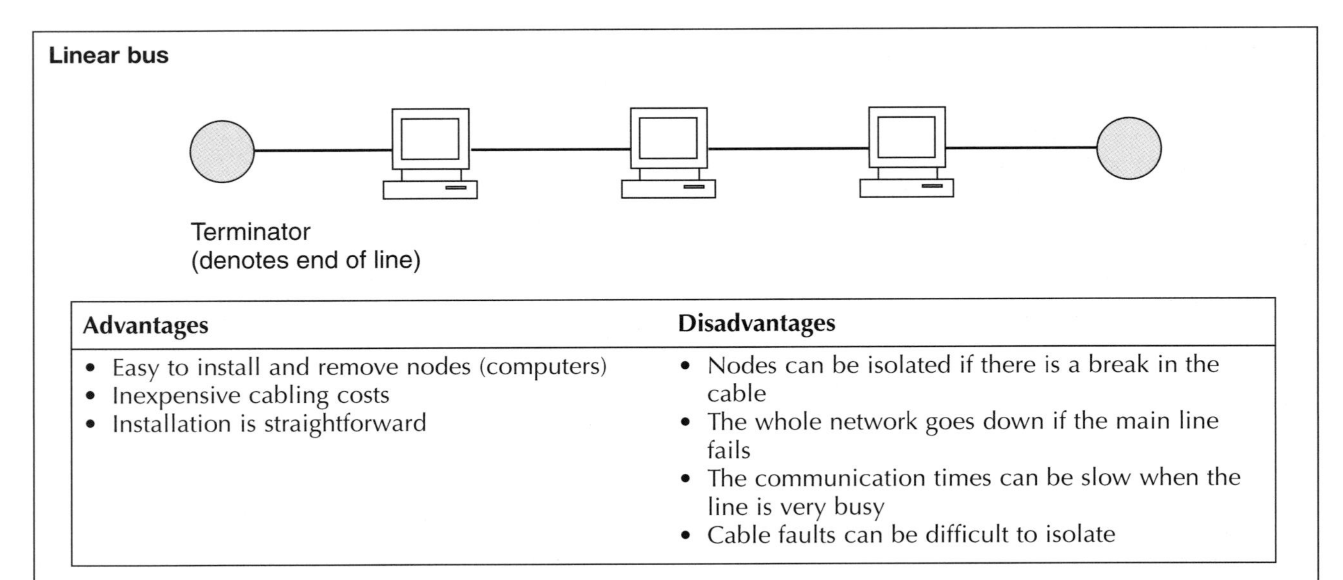

Advantages	Disadvantages
• Easy to install and remove nodes (computers) • Inexpensive cabling costs • Installation is straightforward	• Nodes can be isolated if there is a break in the cable • The whole network goes down if the main line fails • The communication times can be slow when the line is very busy • Cable faults can be difficult to isolate

Bus network

- Uses a single shared cable.
- Data can be transmitted in both directions.
- If two messages are sent at the same time, a collision occurs.
- CSMA/CD (carrier sense multiple access/collision detection) is a protocol used on Ethernet networks to detect and handle collisions.
- Each station checks that the line is not busy before transmitting data. If it is, it waits until the line is free.
- When data is being sent, the terminal listens for other terminals which may also begin transmission.
- If a collision occurs, both terminals abort the transmission and wait a random period of time before trying again.

Note Ethernet can make use of different types of cable but it has a limited distance for each segment (typically 100 m). In order to increase this distance, segments have to be joined together.

Two local area networks can be joined together by using a **bridge**, which is a connection device enabling the two networks to act as one.

Star

Advantages
• Each node has a direct line to the server • High level of security between stations • New nodes can be easily connected • Faults are easier to isolate

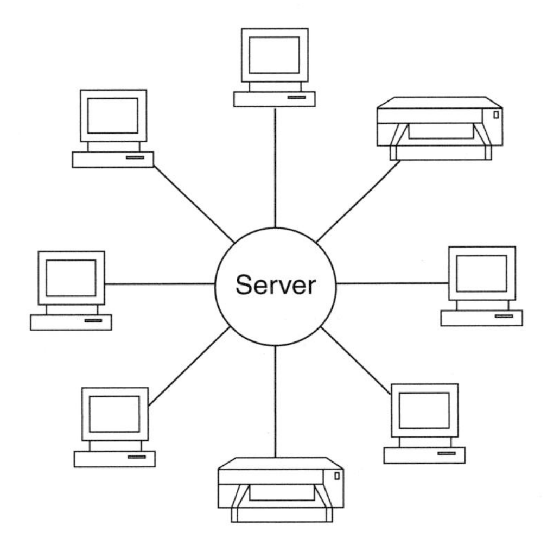

Disadvantages
• A bottleneck at the server can occur at peak times thus slowing down the whole communication process • Cable costs can be expensive since each node has its own direct line to the server • Transmission speeds can vary between devices

Network configurations (continued)

Star network

- Each terminal is connected to the central computer with its own cable.
- The central computer is called the **hub**.
- The hub polls each terminal in turn to establish if they want to send data.
- When data is sent to the hub, it retransmits the data to all other terminals.
- Only the terminal with the destination address processes the data.

Ring

Advantages

- Information is sent in one direction around the ring making communication very straightforward
- Additional nodes can be added
- High speed data transfer
- Each node controls its data transmission

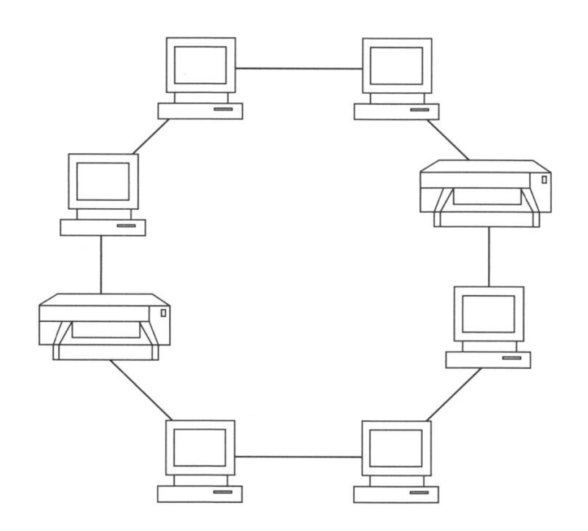

Disadvantages

- If a node fails to operate properly, then the communication system can be disrupted
- Cable faults can be difficult to isolate and can cause the network to go down

Ring network

- Each terminal is connected to the ring.
- A small carrier packet of data called a **token** is passed around the ring in one direction only.
- If a terminal wishes to send data, it attaches to the token the data packet with the address of the sender and the destination address.
- The packet is either taken off the ring at the destination address or it returns to the sender unread, where it is then taken off.
- The token is released onto the ring where it continues to go around waiting for a package to be attached.

The Cambridge ring is a token ring network which has a number of tokens travelling around the ring at fixed time intervals.

Quite often a combination of the above topologies is used in local area networks.

Special software is used with each of the above configurations to ensure the most secure and efficient method of communication.

Protocol stack

The International Standards Organisation (ISO) has established a model to define the ways in which different computer networks are connected to each other. The most common protocol stack is TCP/IP and this follows the Open Systems Interconnections (OSI) guidelines.

OSI seven-layer model

7 Application layer	Provides a link with the user
6 Presentation layer	Deals with how the data is presented in different standard forms: for example, encryption, ASCII and formatting for devices.
5 Session layer	Synchronises data transfer and manages connections between different systems
4 Transport layer	Provides communication features to regulate the flow of data
3 Network layer	Adds routing and address information and deals with data movement and error control
2 Data ink layer	Provides error checking for data and transmission procedures
1 Physical layer	Electrical connections and data in binary form

Multiplexing

Time-division multiplexing (TDM)

Time slice

Multiplexor

High-speed stream of data

Multiplexor

Time slice

- Transmission time is split into small slices and shared between the terminals.
- Each terminal sends data for this fixed period of time in quick succession.
- If the bandwidth is high, then the turns taken by each terminal are very frequent.
- There are no start and stop bits needed since the systems clock synchronises the transfer of the signals.
- The impression is given that all the terminals are sending and receiving the data simultaneously.

Frequency-division multiplexing (FDM)

Circuit-switching networks

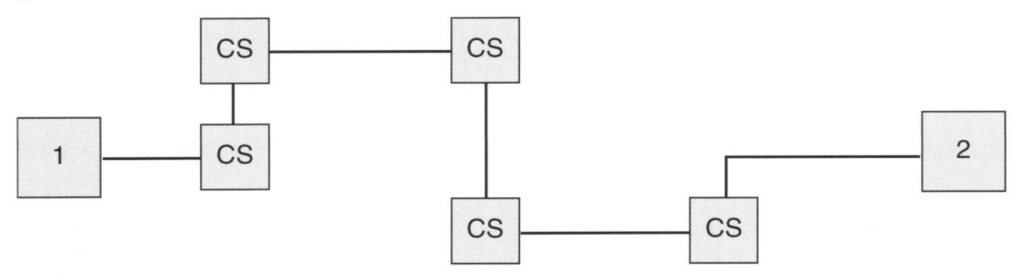

CS Circuit switch

- A dedicated line between two terminals is needed: for example, using the telephone exchange.
- A number of circuit switches are used to establish a route between the two user terminals.
- This network approach is limited in terms of speed and quality of signal.

Packet-switching networks

- Messages are broken down into small chunks called **packets**.
- Used extensively in wide area networks.
- A packet contains: data to be sent; destination address and source address; error control bits; coded information to enable the reassembly of the packets into the original message.
- The packets have a fixed upper limit in size.
- The packets can use different routes and are then assembled into the correct order at their destination.
- This network approach is efficient and is reasonably secure.

Asynchronous transfer mode (ATM)

- Very high transmission speeds.
- A type of packet-switching system (PSS) which supports a variety of data types.
- Uses digital lines, therefore a secure and high-quality signal is achieved.
- Packets are referred to as **cells** and are usually of fixed size.

Sometimes virtual circuits are created with PSS. There are no physical connections made but a transmission pathway is established and agreed on by the sending and receiving terminals. At this point, the actual connection is established.

Many large businesses probably have undergone several major changes to their original computer systems. Hardware and software updates are a regular occurrence and so computer systems will inevitably require some modification from time to time.

In many situations, the traditional systems life cycle is used to assess and implement the necessary changes. There is a number of different stages to this model.

Traditional waterfall/cascade approach

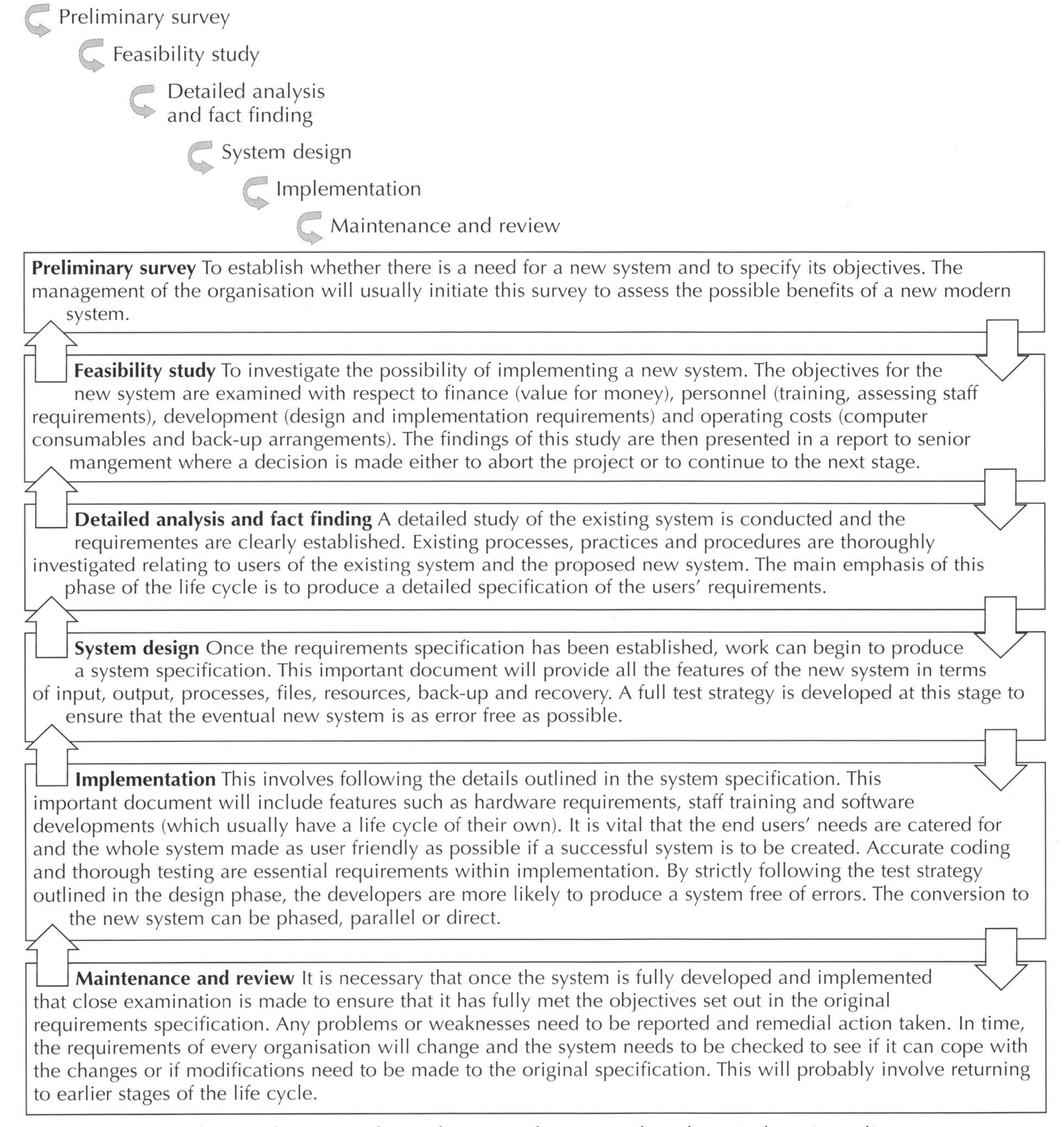

Quite often sections have to be revisited in order to rectify or amend work carried out in earlier stages.

This model is sometimes referred to as the waterfall or cascade approach to systems development and may consist of all or several of the stages listed above. With this method, each stage must be completed before the next one can begin. However, it is not unusual for several phases to be revisited in the light of later ones.

Although this approach is still very popular today, it gives little credence to the end user. For this reason, it is vital that the users' needs are fully investigated and considered in the early stages in order to prevent rejection when considerable time, effort and expense have been given.

Early stages

There is a wide variety of factors that can influence the desire or need to change. Reasons such as:

- The manual system just will not cope with the volume of work.
- The existing system is inefficient due to the poor hardware specification or software version.
- Company procedures and practices have changed.
- The nature of the business had changed from, for example, batch to real time.
- There is mass duplication, etc.

Once a formal request is made with respect to computerisation or updating, then the systems life cycle can begin.

Feasibility study

This is a very important stage in the life cycle because, after considering all the important factors which influence current and future plans, a decision is made either to proceed with the new system or to abort the project. The findings of this study are presented to the management in a report. The report may include:

Operational feasibility This is concerned with how the existing system functions and whether or not similar methods of practice could be used with the new system. The main limiting factor is often the users' reluctance or inability to change.

Technical feasibility This is concerned with the technology required and the technical expertise needed to design, install and eventually use the new system. It considers the existing hardware and expertise.

Financial feasibility This is concerned with the cost effectiveness of the new system. Bank managers believe that every debit should have a credit. If this fails to be a reality over a long time scale, then it is doubtful whether the project will proceed.

Systems analysis

A detailed study of the existing system is carried out along with an in-depth look at the requirements of the new system. A requirements specification is drawn up which identifies the users needs and how they can be effectively met. A variety of methods for gathering and representing the data can be used.

Fact finding methods

Data capture forms (questionnaires)

Provided the questions are carefully planned and are unambiguous, this method of data collection can be very worthwhile. This approach is ideal for gathering information from a large number of people.

Interview

End users at every level within the organisation can be interviewed. This is an ideal method for gathering information since the communication is two way. However, it is very time consuming.

Observation

Snapshots of the organisation are gathered over a period of time. End users are monitored and existing practices, time scales and interaction between people and departments are observed in the real working environment. Problems and difficulties are noted and can hopefully be rectified in the new system.

Inspecting existing documents/files

How things are done at present and the volumes of data used (or needed) form the main focus of this method of fact finding. Documents can be analysed on site or taken away for a more detailed examination.

Systems analysis (continued)

Data flow diagram (DFD)

One of the major challenges facing the systems analyst is to establish how data and information move around a system. Data flow diagrams can be used to help represent this movement in a diagrammatic way. The symbols used are:

This represents an external data source (for example, an order form) or data destination source (for example, an invoice).

This represents a process: that is, an operation performed on the data.

This represents a data store which is used to collect the data of a similar type.

This represents data flow. The arrow should be labelled to help describe what is happening.

DFDs are often drawn to represent the data flow, at first in a general sense and then in more detail as different stages or levels are produced. The top level is called a **level 0 diagram** or **top level diagram**. Each level of detail is numbered in sequence: that is, level 1, then level 2.

This level 0 (or top level) DFD shows the main sources of data for a customer involved in placing an order for stock items from a company.

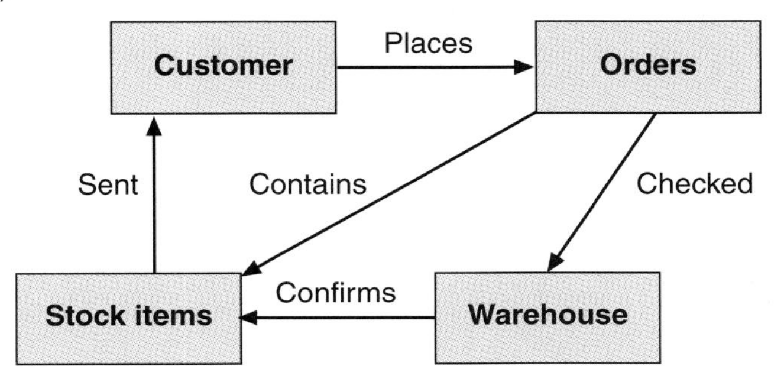

This DFD considers the requirements for a customer wanting to place an order for items of stock. The order is placed, checked and validated. If it is correct, the stock file is checked to clarify whether the items are in stock. To process the order, the price is worked out and the relevant files are updated. An invoice is sent to the customer and a despatch note is sent to the warehouse.

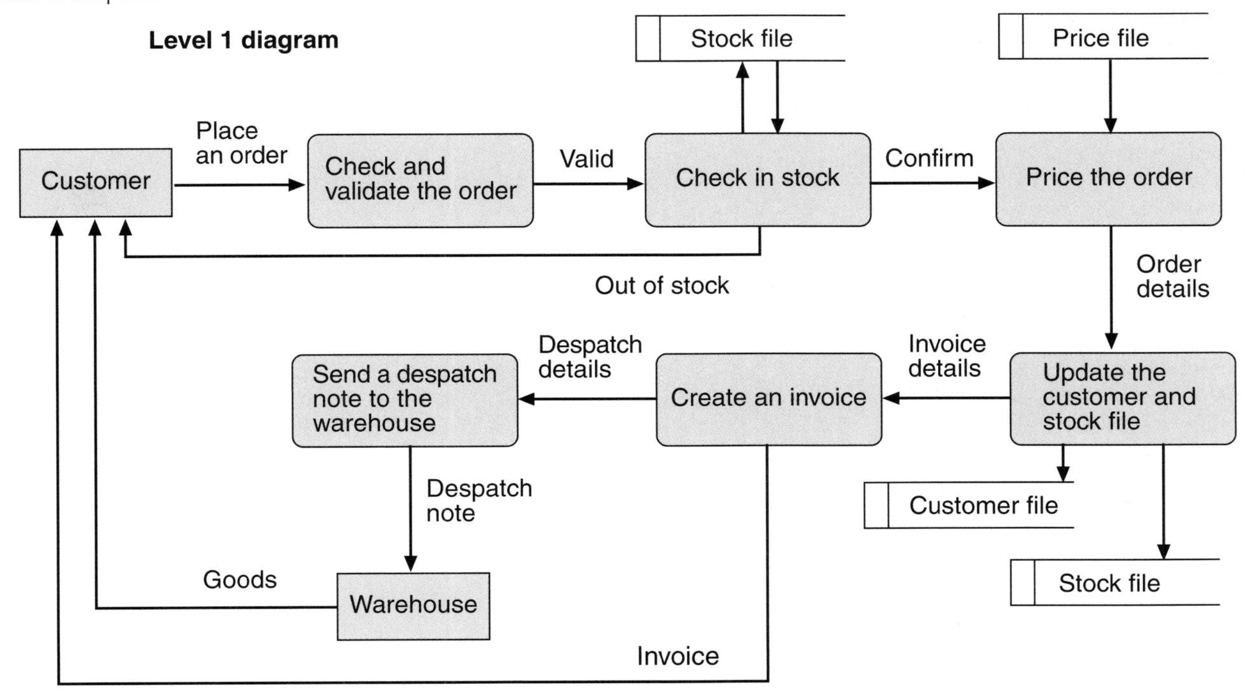

Design phase

During this phase in the lifecycle, the systems analyst would consider a variety of alternative designs which match the **requirements specification**. Eventually, a **systems specification** is drawn up which provides detailed documentation of the new system.

System specification contents

Outline information

- Outline of project.
- Contents lists.
- Names of people and departments involved.
- Personnel responsible for various sections.

Aims and objectives

The project will be divided up into sections and a brief description of what is expected of the new system will be stated.

Specification details

- I/O documents.
- File details.
- Storage requirements and methods.
- Program details and test data.
- Timetable of events for hardware and software.
- Changeover procedures.

Computer equipment

- A full list and description of all the hardware.
- Installation and maintenance details.
- Human computer interaction.

Summary

Design features

Some of the factors which need to be considered by the analyst during this phase are:

Input

- Careful design of the data collection methods needed.
- Volume of data expected.
- Validation methods.

Output

- This will greatly affect the input design. Reports and documents needed. Media such as screen output or hard copy needs careful consideration.

Files

- Record/data structure.
- Organisation and access methods.
- Storage medium.

Software

- Diagrams to show the data flow.
- Reusable procedures and modules.
- Suite of programs.
- Choice of testing strategies.

User interface

This can use menus, commands, icons or a combination. Good clear screen layouts are essential with help facilities on hand. The navigation should be clear. The needs of the user have to be carefully considered.

Security

The data has to be kept safe from accidental or deliberate tampering.

Design phase (continued)

Design methods

The design methods given below can be used in a variety of computing situations. In the life cycle, they are used to very good effect in the creation of programs and testing.

Top down design

This method starts with a general description of the task and then subdivides into sections which add more detail. The lowest level represents the most specific modules.

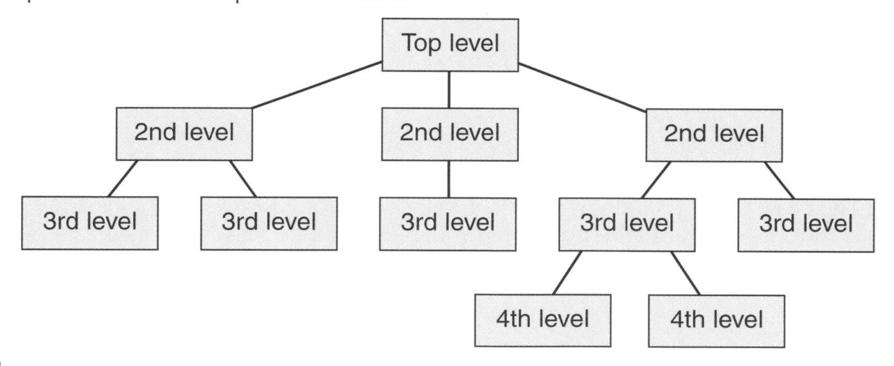

Bottom up design

This method starts at the lowest level with modules or procedures and then joins them to create the next level up. By progressively combining segments, the top level is achieved.

Program and system design

- A selection of charts, tables and diagrams can be used to specify the programs needed for a new system
- System design includes the hardware components, while program design deals mainly with the flow of data in a software setting
- **Algorithms** can be used to good effect to specify instructions. An algorithm is a step-by-step set of instructions to solve a given task. (See page 92.)
- The **pseudo-code** is the intermediate stage between natural language (that is, English) and the programming language. In a shorthand way, it describes how the solution to a task is to be achieved using technical language.

Prototyping

This is an approach used by designers to help them and their target audience experience the suggested ideas and give feedback on possible alterations. In certain situations, the prototype is discarded and the main system is developed using the main guidelines, principles and practices. However, in other situations, the prototype can evolve into the final system. With this approach to design, the end user is more likely to get a greater say in the eventual system and hence more likely to accept it fully.

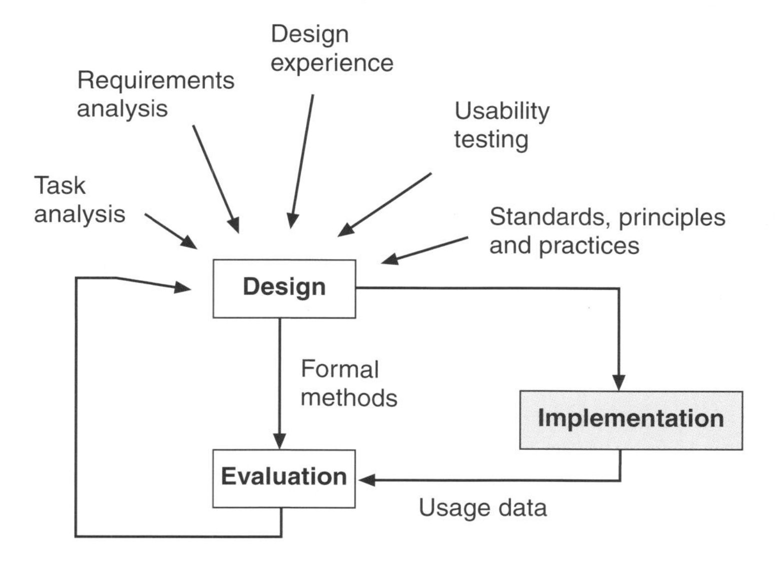

Coding

This is usually carried out by a team of programmers in accordance with the system specification. The programming team are usually responsible for writing the code, testing each section of it, writing and producing the user documentation and working with the analyst to amend or alter the programs as needed.

Testing

This is a very important phase in the life cycle. Every effort is made to ensure that all aspects of the system perform properly and meet with the expectations of the designers and end users. A variety of strategies and approaches are used to try to cover every eventuality.

In the development of any new computer system, the software must undergo rigorous testing before it is available for operational release.

Unit testing Each component is tested separately with suitable test data to ensure that it functions properly and as required.

Integration testing A number of components are tested together to ensure that they interact correctly to produce the desired response.

System testing Using suitable test data, the whole system is tested to ensure that all the parts function correctly and meet the specification outcomes.

Acceptance testing The programs are finally tested with real data in the environment where they will eventually be used. A number of end users can put the program through its paces to ensure it meets their expectations with relation to speed, ease of use, volume of data, consistency, etc.

Dry run

One of the techniques used by the programmer to ensure that individual modules of a program work correctly is to use a **dry run**. This involves working through a section of code manually to try to locate any errors.

A trace table is constructed from the program listing and variables are tracked as the instructions are executed. Testing in this way does not require a computer and it helps to give the programmer a clearer idea of what is happening at each line in the code.

Test data

As the program is written, the various sections are usually tested with preset test data. This could include:

- Mid-range valid data to ensure that the program can function correctly with the majority of expected values.
- Extreme-range valid data to test the program at its upper and lower limits.
- Invalid data to ensure that the program can handle it without crashing. Suitable messages are usually generated informing the user that the data, operation or process is invalid.

Program testing

A number of different strategies can be used to help ensure the program works correctly.

Top-down testing

The various branches of the complete system are tested. Eventually each component is tested and interrelationships checked.

Bottom-up testing

Individual modules are tested as they are written and combined to form larger units which are then tested together. Eventually the whole system is tested.

Functional testing

This type of test (Black Box) is used to ensure that the program can function properly with all the different types of test data.

Logical testing

This type of test (White Box) attempts to examine *all* the paths that are available in the program. For example, if a program has several branches in a certain module, then all branches are investigated to ensure the program works correctly.

Once a system has been fully developed and tested rigorously in a variety of different ways, it still has to undergo a few more tests.

Alpha testing

This method of testing software is restricted to a small group of users within the developer's own company. This alpha test is usually the first of two final tests on the software and can help to find any errors or omissions in the earlier life-cycle phases.

Beta testing

The software is almost ready for general release. The results of the alpha test have been carefully scrutinized and any necessary changes have been made to the software. A number of potential users are now given the opportunity to try out this beta version of the software and provide constructive comments. Provided the feedback is mainly positive and glaring inadequacies are found, the software is prepared for final launch.

Implementation

In the transition from the old system to the new, a number of issues have to be carefully coordinated.

Hardware Modifications to existing buildings or a complete rebuild needs to be considered. Furniture, room layout, wiring and heating are some of the features that need consideration.

Software Network, applications and bespoke programs are installed and checked to ensure they all work as required.

Files All the necessary data is installed onto the new system. These could be manual files or old computer files that require conversion and updating. The volume of the data could cause a problem if it was not tested for during the previous phase.

Training The staff have to be made aware of how the new software works. Becoming familiar with a new computer system requires time and much patience.

One of the major aspects of the implementation phase is deciding on a changeover strategy.

Direct changeover

This is where the new system completely replaces the old without overlapping. The main difficulty with this method is when the new system fails to operate as expected, thus leaving the staff in limbo.

Parallel changeover

The old system works alongside the new for a short period of time. Comparisons can be made and results checked to ensure that the new system is functioning correctly.

Pilot running

A section of the organisation is computerised and tried out in an experimental fashion alongside the manual system. Results can be compared and checked to ensure the new system works correctly. This approach is useful when finance is a major factor and sometimes total computerisation is not needed immediately and so it can be examined on a smaller scale.

Phased changeover

Sections of an organisation can be computerised while others remain unchanged. This method facilitates training and financing. Sometimes the technology is not at a sufficiently advanced stage for a section of the organisation to benefit from complete computerisation and this phased approach is adopted.

Whatever way the new system is implemented, training is an essential element if the technology is to be fully utilised.

Installation manuals These documents tell the user how to install the software and set up the system.

User manuals These will probably cater for a range of end users: for example, management, general staff, competent computer users and novices. The documentation will basically instruct the user on how the software works and is usually divided into a number of related sections for ease of reference.

Operations manuals These documents will provide information for the technical users. How to use the hardware components and ensure backup and recovery are among the sections covered.

Training This information is usually provided in a variety of ways, for example: video; instruction from a tutor; on-line tutoring; training documents/manuals; use of technical support team.

Often a combination of the above approaches is brought together to make the learning experience more enjoyable and beneficial.

Maintenance and review

In time, any new system will need to be updated and certainly maintained if it is to function effectively and meet the needs of the organisation. Technical documentation is often provided to help facilitate the regular maintenance of the system. Any alterations to the original specification are carried out by specialist staff and not by end users.

Adaptive maintenance The system may need to be modified to deal with new legislation or changes in organisational procedures. New hardware may require some changes to the software so that it can be fully utilised.

Corrective maintenance If errors are found in the system, some minor changes may need to be made to resolve the problems and prevent further problems.

Perfective maintenance Even at this stage in the life cycle, changes can still be made if it helps to make the system more efficient and enhance the overall performance.

If the system is well designed, then the maintenance of the system should be easier. This is the challenge that each design team face every time they begin a new system.

An evaluation of any new system is usually carried out on the basis of effectiveness, usability and maintainability.

Algorithms are step-by-step instructions to solve specific tasks. In order to write good, structured algorithms, the user must fully understand the processes involved in the task. In addition to this, a sound understanding of the basic programming constructs is needed so that the algorithm can be written in a reasonable pseudo-code.

Algorithm tips

Indentation

It is very useful to indent algorithms and code to help show where one loop or condition starts and ends. For example:

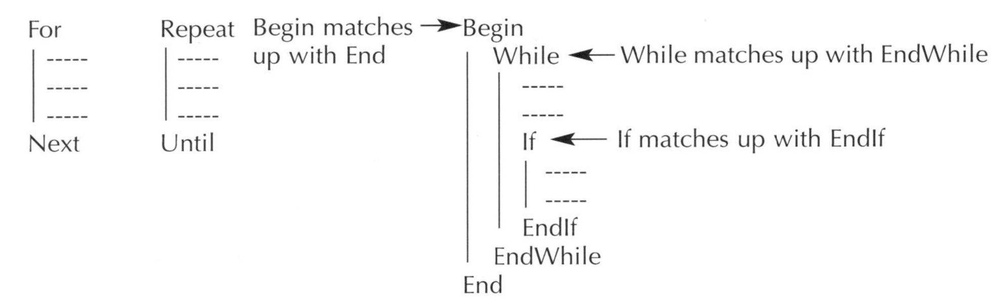

Assignment

Many treat these statements as pure mathematical signs but they are not. For example:

count = count +1

If 'count = 6 'at start
then 'count = current value +1'
So 'count' is 6 + 1 = 7

This means get the variable called 'count' and add 1 to it. Then place this new result back into the variable 'count.'

Sometimes it is written like this:

count :=count + 1
or count ←———— count +1

They are the same thing, basically telling the program to place the result of the right-hand side into the variable on the left-hand side.

Below are some standard assignment convention short forms.

```
num1 += num2;  // This is equal to num1 = num1 + num2
num1 -= num2;  // This is equal to num1 = num1 - num2
num1 *= num2;  // This is equal to num1 = num1 * num2
num1 /= num2;  // This is equal to num1 = num1 / num2
```

Arrays

An array is generally thought of as a group of data items with a common name which are distinguished one from the other using a subscripted variable. The array is usually Dimensioned (declared)at the beginning of the program to inform the computer to reserve space for the array values.

Take, for example an array containing five names:

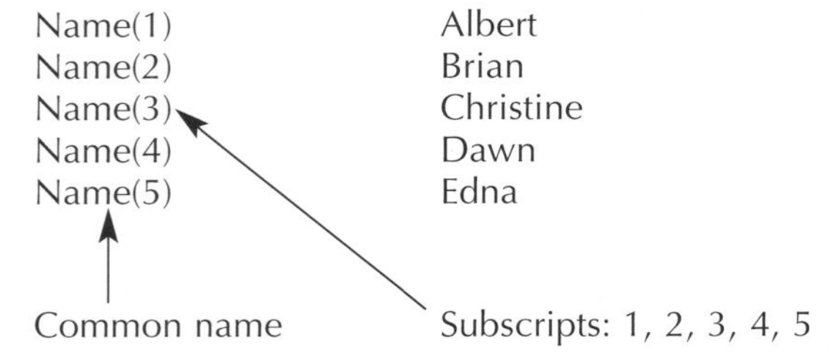

Using the array, the values can be swapped around or searched for with relative ease.

The following algorithms and methods are the main ones used for computing at A-level. However, the skills needed here are relevant to creating algorithms for any computer related task.

Searching

Linear search
This is a fairly simple technique where each item in a list is examined one at a time in sequential order.

```
Begin
    Identify the data item to be searched for           This will eventually change if
    Set found = False  ---------------------------->    a match is found
        While there is data in the list Do                       |
            Read data item from the list                         |
            If a match is found Then                             |
                Write details of match                           |
                found = True  <----------------------------------
            Endif
        EndWhile
End
If found = False Then write 'No match found'
```

This algorithm could be refined further to move it closer to a target language. But in this format, it helps to identify some of the algorithmic features.

Binary split search
This is a much more efficient searching method than the previous one. However, with this method the data items have to be in order.

Consider an array called Word of *n* items, where H is highest value, L is lowest value and M is median value.

Array	Method
Word (1)	1 Ensure that the words are in alphabetical order.
Word (2)	2 Let low=first value (1) and high = last value (*n*)

-----	3 Calculate the median value by adding high and low valuers then dividing by 2.
Word (*n*)	

Array	Method
H -----	

----- M found ←	4 If the median value is the Searchword being searched for, then search ends.

L -----	
H -----	

----- M Replace M with L ←	If the Searchword is larger than the median value, then let low = median value.
----- Discard bottom part	
L -----	
H -----	
----- Discard top part ←	If the Searchword is less than the median word, then let high = median value.
----- M Replace M with H	

L -----	
	5 With the new value of high or low, repeat steps 3–5 until Word is found.
	6 If the word is not found, then report it as missing.

Searching (continued)

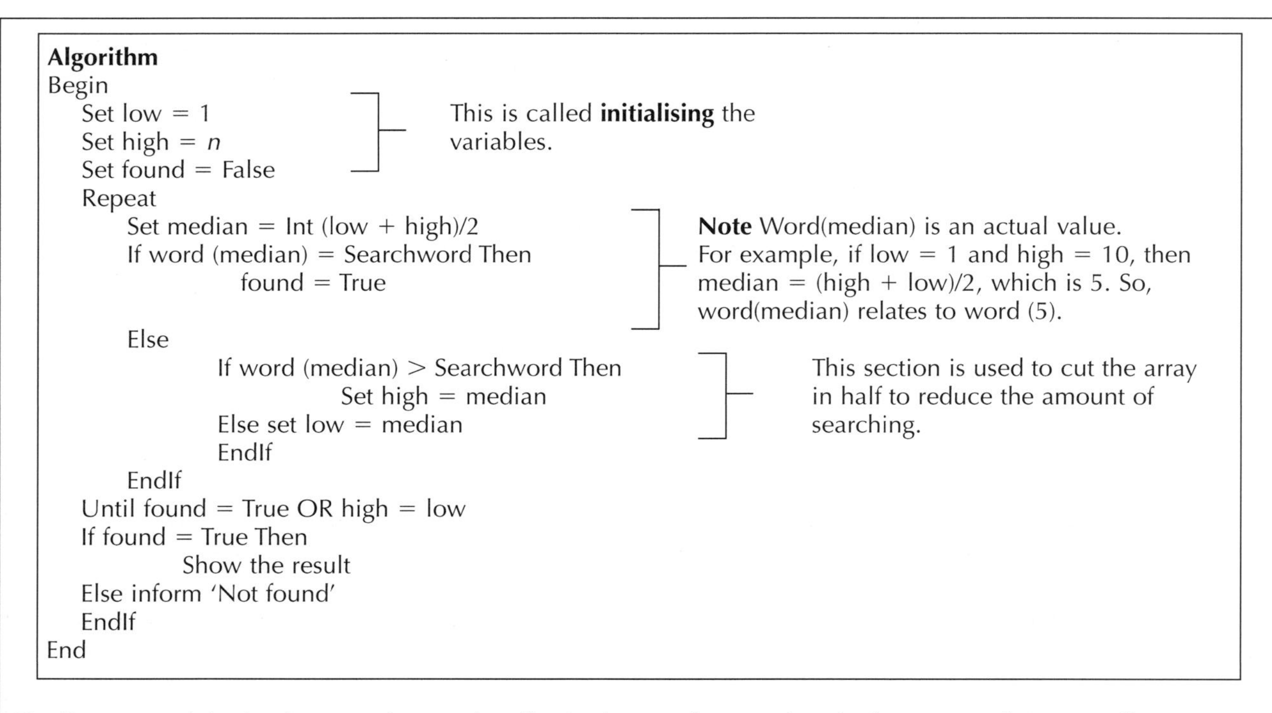

Algorithm

```
Begin
    Set low = 1              ┐
    Set high = n             ├  This is called initialising the
    Set found = False        ┘  variables.
    Repeat
        Set median = Int (low + high)/2              ┐ Note Word(median) is an actual value.
        If word (median) = Searchword Then           ├ For example, if low = 1 and high = 10, then
                found = True                         │ median = (high + low)/2, which is 5. So,
                                                     ┘ word(median) relates to word (5).
        Else
                If word (median) > Searchword Then    ┐ This section is used to cut the array
                        Set high = median             ├ in half to reduce the amount of
                Else set low = median                 ┘ searching.
                EndIf
        EndIf
    Until found = True OR high = low
    If found = True Then
            Show the result
    Else inform 'Not found'
    EndIf
End
```

The linear search is simple to produce and well suited to small arrays, but the binary search is very efficient especially with large arrays.

To find a specific matchstick in an unsorted pile is extremely difficult if not impossible, particularly when the pile is very large.

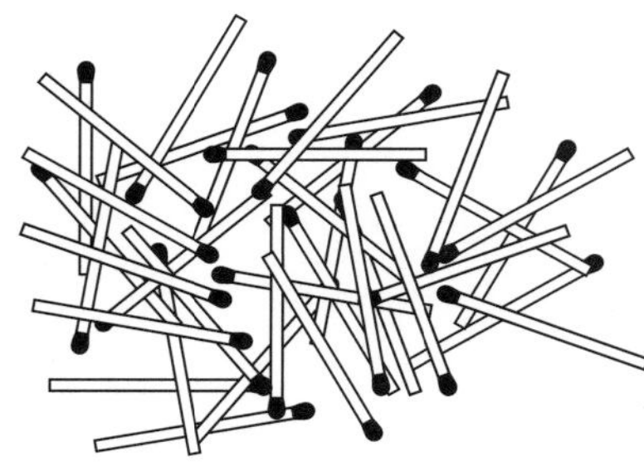

When the pile is ordered, a search becomes possible and easier to administer. Several different methods could be used – some more efficient than others.

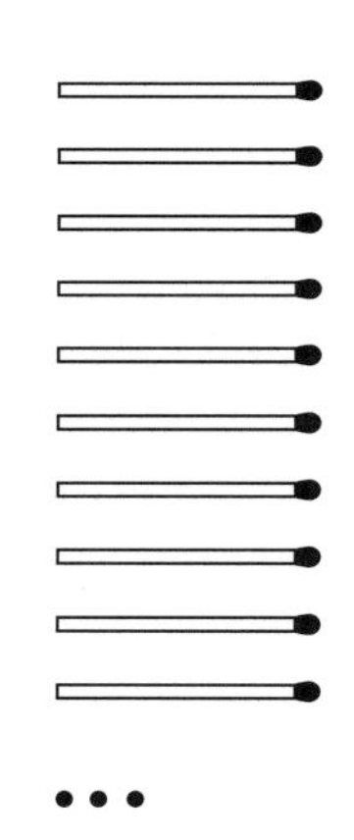

Sorting

Sorting is a technique that is used extensively in computing. There are a large number of different methods for sorting values into ascending or descending sequence. The **bubble sort** (also known as the **swap sort**) will be exemplified.

Bubble sort

This method (for ascending order) involves the following procedure.

- Compare the first pair of values. If the first is larger than the second, swap them.
- Compare the second value in the array with the third. If the second is larger than the third, swap them.
- Repeat this until the last pair: that is, the $(n-1)$th term is compared with the nth term (the one before the last and the last term).

Note There are $(n-1)$ pairs of values to compare in any array. For example, in a six number array, five comparisons (pairs of values) are made when trying to put six values in order.

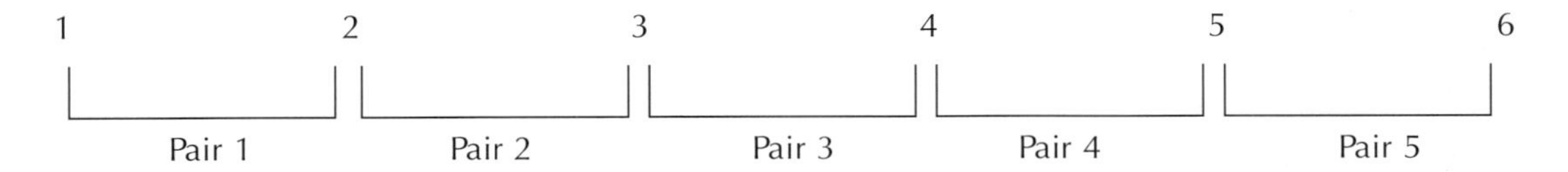

If no swaps were made during the above process, then the numbers are in order. However, if any swaps were made, the whole process is usually carried out again until there is none.

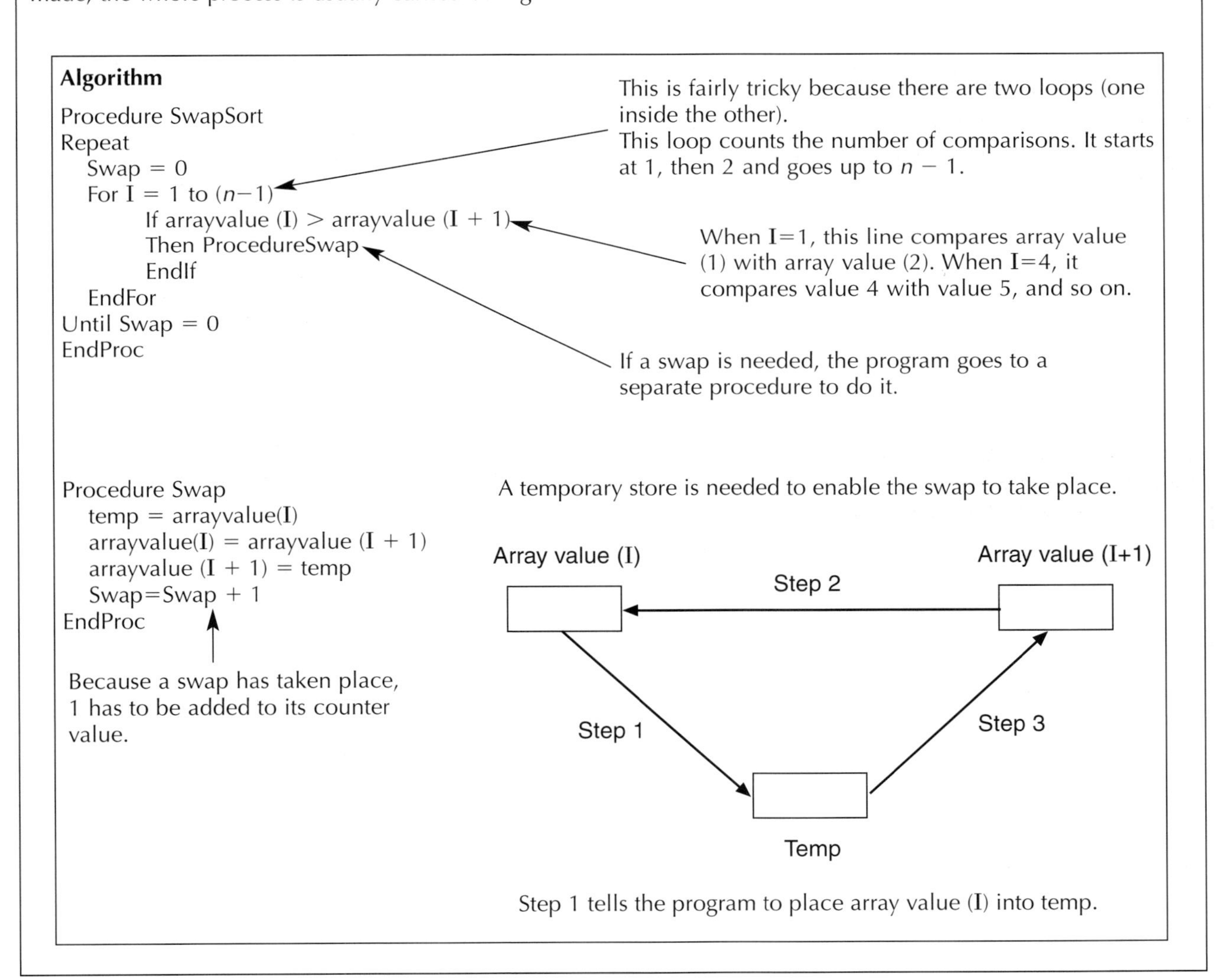

Stacks

Pushing an element onto a stack
The method consists of the following.

- Check if the stack is full.
- If not, increase the current top value by 1.
- Change the stack pointer to point to the new data item.

Algorithm
```
Procedure Push
        If topvalue = Max Then
                Print 'Full'
        Else topvalue = topvalue + 1
                Stack(topvalue) = new item
        EndIf
EndProcedure
```

Popping an element from a stack
The method consists of the following.

- Check if the stack is empty.
- If not, pop the data off the stack.
- Decrease the current top value by 1.

Algorithm
```
Procedure Pop
        If topvalue = 0 Then
                Print 'Empty'
        Else poppeditem = Stack(topvalue)
                Topvalue = topvalue −1
        EndIf
EndProcedure
```

Queues

Linear queues

1	2	3	4	5	6	7	8

Adding a new element to a queue (pushing)
The method consists of the following.

- Data is entered at the back of the queue and leaves from the front hence the fifo data structure (first in first out).
- Check if the queue is empty. If so, add a value.
- Check if it is full. If so, report queue as full.
- If not one of the above, then add the value at the back of the queue.

Variables used

maxsize	Maximum number of items that can be held in the queue.
items in queue	This is an array value. For example, arrayvalue(3) means three items in the queue.
front	The first item in the queue.
back	The last item in the queue.
dataitem	The values that make up the queue.

Algorithm
```
If the queue is empty Then
        front=1
        back=1
        arrayvalue(back)=dataitem
Else
        If back=maxsize Then
                Print 'Queue Full'
        Else back=back+1
                arrayvalue(back)=dataitem
        EndIf
EndIf
```

Queues (continued)

Deleting an element from a queue (popping)
The method consists of the following.

- Check if the queue is empty. If so, stop.
- If not empty, get data from the front of the queue.
- Check if there is only one item in the queue then reset the variables.
- If more than one item, then take one from the front and adjust the front pointer.

Algorithm
```
If items in the queue=0 Then
        Print 'Queue Empty'
Else
        datavalue=arrayvalue(front)
        If front=back Then
                front=0
                back=0
        Else
                front=front+1
        EndIf
EndIf
```

Circular queues
The above algorithms are for linear queues but more often than not queues are circular in nature. This means that when data items are removed from the front, this vacant space can be reused. With minor alterations, these algorithms could be modified to suit a circular queue format.

Lists

Printing the elements of a list of names
Method recursion is used so that the procedure calls itself until the list is complete.

While the list is not empty, print the Head of the list, remove the Head from the list and let the Tail become the new list.

Algorithm
```
Procedure Name(list)
        If the list is not Empty(list) Then
                Print (Head(list))
                Name(Tail(list))
        EndIf
EndProc
```

Trace tables are useful to show the results of each cell.

If the names in the list were Name(Andrew, Ben, Catherine, David, Ewan), then the above algorithm would produce:

Recursive order	List	Printout
1	[Andrew, Ben, Catherine, David, Ewan]	Andrew
2	[Ben, Catherine, David, Ewan]	Ben
3	[Catherine, David, Ewan]	Catherine
4	[David, Ewan]	David
5	[Ewan]	Ewan
6	[ ]	

A-Level revision questions

1 Applications

1 List three different Acts of Parliament relating to computing.

2 Distinguish between data subjects and data users.

3 Identify five different principles set out by the Data Protection Act about data users.

4 What are the main reasons behind the 1988 and 1990 Acts?

5 Describe the key features of a word processing package.

6 Outline the main features of a spreadsheet package.

7 Explain the key features of a database package.

8 What is DTP and what are the main features of this software?

9 How has computerisation affected employment and the nature of the work, over the past 30 years?

10 Describe three different health and safety issues realting to computing.

11 What is AI and how is it being used with computers?

12 Describe the main features of an expert system.

13 Distinguish clearly between CAD, CAM and CAL.

14 Why is the principle of feedback so important to computers using control applications?

15 Describe three different examples of computer simulation.

16 What is the Internet and why has it made such a dramatic impact on all aspects of modern life?

17 Describe six different features of the Internet.

A-Level revision questions

2 Input, output and storage

1 What are peripheral devices?

2 Select any five input devices and try to get pictures and further information about them using the Internet.

3 Distinguish between an ink jet and a laser printer.

4 What is COM? Describe the advantages and disadvantages of using this form of output.

5 Describe two types of graph plotter and explain the distinguishing features of each.

6 Describe a situation where a graph plotter would be used for output.

7 Describe the main features of a VDU.

8 Many modern computers don't have a floppy drive. Why do you think this is the case?

9 Distinguish between a hard disc and a zip disc in terms of capacity and use.

10 Define the following terms: CD ROM, DVD, WORM. Suggest an application where each would be used.

11 Why is tape still used today as a valid medium for storing data?

12 Distinguish clearly between a tape streamer and DAT. Suggest a suitable application where each would be used to good effect.

A-Level revision questions

3 Data representation

1. Define the terms 'bit', 'byte' and 'word'.
2. Describe several different coding systems and state clearly why they are needed.
3. Distinguish between denary, binary, octal and hexadecimal.
4. Convert the following denary (base 10) numbers into binary (base 2): 37, 23, 46.
5. Convert the following denary (base 10) numbers into octal (base 8): 89, 67, 76.
6. Convert the following denary (base 10) numbers into hexadecimal (base 16): 134, 108, 170.
7. Represent the following decimal base 10 numbers in binary: 19.25, 9.5, 23.3125.
8. Show how BCD would be used to represent the numbers 0–9.
9. Distinguish clearly between analogue and digital signals.
10. Define the term 'resolution' and distinguish between high and low resolution.
11. Distinguish between data and information.
12. Distinguish between direct and indirect methods of gathering and using data.
13. Show how the following calculations would be performed using two's complement: 35 – 20, 26 – 19.
14. Represent the following numbers in sign and magnitude notation: 37, 23, −40, −13.
15. Distinguish clearly between fixed and floating point as methods of representing numbers.
16. Clearly state the purpose of the mantissa and the exponent in fixed and floating point notation.
17. Show how the numbers 3.5 and −3.5 can be represented in normalised floating point notation.

A-Level revision questions

4 Operating systems

1 What are the functions of an operation system?

2 Distinguish between a program file and a data file.

3 What are the main duties of the file manager section of the operation system?

4 Define the term 'pathname'.

5 How is it possible to have two files with the same name saved on a computer?

6 Describe the term 'access rights'.

7 Why is it so important to have back-up and archive files?

8 What are the main responsibilities of the input/output management section of the operation system?

9 What is a loader program? Describe three different types.

10 Distinguish between virtual memory and paging.

11 What are DLLs and what is their purpose?

12 Briefly describe three different processing states.

13 What is scheduling and why is it used?

14 Describe four different interface types used with human–computer interaction.

A-Level revision questions

5 Machine architecture

1 What are the three main parts of the CPU?

2 Describe the three main types of bus used in the CPU.

3 Define the term 'interface'.

4 What is meant by the term 'fetch–decode–execute' cycle?

5 Describe how an arithmetic operation is fetched, decoded and executed.

6 Describe how a logical operation is fetched, decoded and executed.

7 What is a register?

8 Describe the following registers: CIR, SCR, MAR, MDR, Acc, PSR

9 What is an interrupt? Describe three different types of interrupt.

10 Describe five ways in which the performance of a computer is affected.

11 Distinguish between M/C and assembly language.

12 Explain the following instruction formats: 3 address; 2 address; 1.5 address; 1 address; zero address.

13 Explain the following methods of addressing: direct, indirect, immediate, indexed, base register.

14 Explain, using suitable examples, the difference between the logical operator AND and OR.

15 Distinguish between conditional and unconditional branch instructions.

16 Explain, using a byte, the following types of shift instruction: logical, cyclic, arithmetic.

17 Distinguish between a macro instruction and a directive.

A-Level revision questions

6 Programming concepts

1 Why were high-level languages developed?

2 Describe the following high-level languages: BASIC, COBOL, Pascal, FORTRAN, PROLOG.

3 Distinguish between 'If . . then' and 'case' as methods of selection.

4 Distinguish between the following iterative structures: While (Do) . . . Endwhile; Repeat . . . Until; For . . . Next (End For).

5 What is an assignment statement? Give four examples.

6 Distinguish between procedure and functions.

7 What is a parameter and describe a suitable situation where parameters can be used to good effect?

8 Explain the features of a block structured program.

9 Distinguish between a local and global variable.

10 Define the term 'recursion'.

11 Briefly describe four generations of computer language.

12 Describe the main features of the following languages: imperative (procedural), declarative, object oriented.

13 Define the following programming terms: 'encapsulation', 'inheritance', 'polymorphism', 'containment', 'class and subclass'.

14 What is translation software and why is it needed?

15 Describe the main features of an assembler. Explain the difference between a one and a two pass assembler.

16 Distinguish between an interpreter and a compiler.

17 Describe the three stages of compilation.

18 Define the term 'syntax' and explain several features of developing a new language.

A-Level revision questions

7 Data structures

1 List five different data structures.

2 What is a list?

3 Distinguish clearly between the head and the tail of a list.

4 Define the term lifo relating to a stack.

5 Explain the terms 'push' and 'pop'.

6 What is a queue and why is it referred to as a fifo data structure?

7 Define the term 'binary tree' and describe the various data elements in the ancestry.

8 Create a binary tree to store the following letters, P, D, T, I, J, S, X, B.

9 Draw a table to show how the letters in Question 8 are linked to each other using a system of pointers.

10 Briefly describe the following methods of traversing a binary tree: preorder, inorder, postorder.

11 Using the following binary tree, show how the tree is traversed using the methods in Question 10.

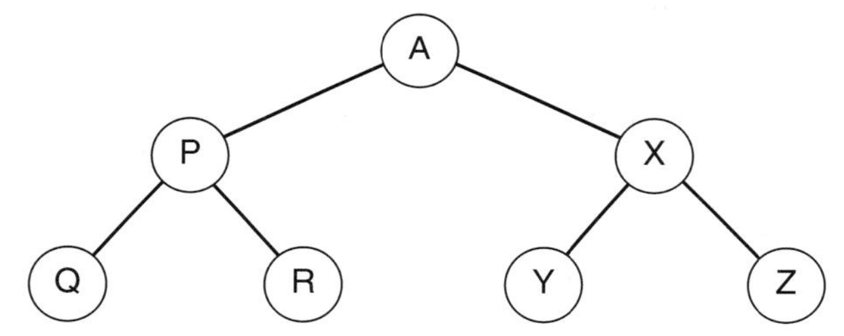

12 Define the term 'static data structure'.

13 Describe the following dynamic data structures: records, files, pointers.

14 What is a linked list?

15 Pointers are used to very good effect with linked lists. Show how pointers could be used to represent and store the following data in alphabetical order:

Name(1) Ewan
Name(2) Joe
Name(3) Catherine
Name(4) Sameer
Name(5) Ben

16 Change the pointer system in Question 15 to: Add Mark, Delete Joe.

A-Level revision questions

8 Files

1 Explain the terms 'database', 'file', 'record' and 'field'.

2 What is a key field and why is it so important?

3 Distinguish between fixed and variable length records.

4 Distinguish between text and non-text files.

5 What are file extensions and why are they used?

6 Describe the content and purpose of the following file types: master file, transaction file, reference file.

7 Draw a table to show a typical file structure for students attending a youth organisation.

8 Distinguish between physical and logical records.

9 What is meant by the term 'hit rate'?

10 Describe how records are added, deleted and edited using the following file organisations: serial, sequential, index sequential, direct (random).

11 Describe four different operations performed on files.

12 Explain the grandfather, father, son principle.

13 Describe how two files stored on tape can be merged to become one.

14 Describe some of the dangers facing an organisation to keep their data secure.

15 Describe the physical, software and complete system failure safeguards used by organisations to keep their data safe.

16 What is data integrity?

17 Describe six different validation checks.

A-Level revision questions

9 Databases

1 What were the factors which led to many businesses using a database to store their data?

2 What is a database and how can it be used effectively by many departments within an organisation?

3 Distinguish between multi-user and object-oriented database systems.

4 What is ODBC?

5 Define the term 'DBMS' and describe some of its functions.

6 What is a DBA and what are his/her duties?

7 Define terms 'schema' and 'subschema'. Describe three different aspects of the schema.

8 What is a data dictionary and why is it so important in database systems?

9 Explain the following terms: DDL, DML, SQL.

10 Distinguish between entitles and attributes.

11 Describe, using relevant examples, the following relationship types: one–one, one–many, many–many.

12 Briefly describe three different database models.

13 Distinguish between the following keys as used in a relational database: primary, composite, foreign.

14 What is meant by the term 'normalised data'? State the three stages of normalisation.

15 Normalise the following order file:

ORDER(Order#, Customer#, Customer – Name, Customer – Address, (Product#, Product – Description, Quantity, Price))

A-Level revision questions

10 Data communication and networks

1. Distinguish between serial and parallel data transmission.
2. What is meant by the term 'bandwidth'?
3. Distinguish between synchronous and asynchronous data transmission.
4. What is parity and why is it needed in a computer system?
5. Define the term 'handshaking'.
6. Describe three different modes of data transmission.
7. Explain the terms FTP and TCP/IP.
8. Describe four different methods of data communication.
9. What is a modem and why is it not needed when an ISDN line is used?
10. Distinguish between public line and private (or leased) line use.
11. Define the term 'ADSL'.
12. What is a network? State some advantages and disadvantages of networking.
13. Distinguish between a WAN and a LAN.
14. What are value added networks?
15. Distinguish between peer-to-peer and server-based networking.
16. Describe in as much detail as you can the features of a linear bus network topology.
17. What is a star network and what are its advantages and disadvantages.
18. Describe in detail the features of a ring network configuration.
19. What is a multiplexor?
20. Explain the terms TDM and FDM relating to multiplexing.
21. Briefly describe the seven layers of the protocol stack.

A-Level revision questions

11 Systems life cycle

1 Briefly describe the main stages in the traditional waterfall/cascade systems life cycle.

2 Describe several features of a feasibility study.

3 Describe four different methods of fact finding and state their advantages and disadvantages.

4 What are DFDs and why are they so useful in systems analysis?

5 Draw a DFD to show the stages involved in booking a holiday.

6 Distinguish between the requirements specification and the systems specification.

7 Briefly describe the contents of a typical systems specification.

8 Describe the factors which need to be considered during the design phase.

9 Distinguish between top down and bottom up design methods.

10 Distinguish between evolutionary and throwaway prototypes.

11 Describe three different approaches used in testing a system.

12 Describe the following testing strategies: top-down, bottom-up, black box, white box.

13 New software takes a long time to develop and undergoes rigorous testing. Two of the final tests on the software are alpha and beta tests. Explain these tests.

14 Describe four different changeover strategies used in systems development.

15 Briefly describe several types of manual that are provided with a new computer system.

16 Describe three different methods of training users how to use a new computerised system.

17 Define the term 'maintenance' relating to a computer system.

A-Level revision questions

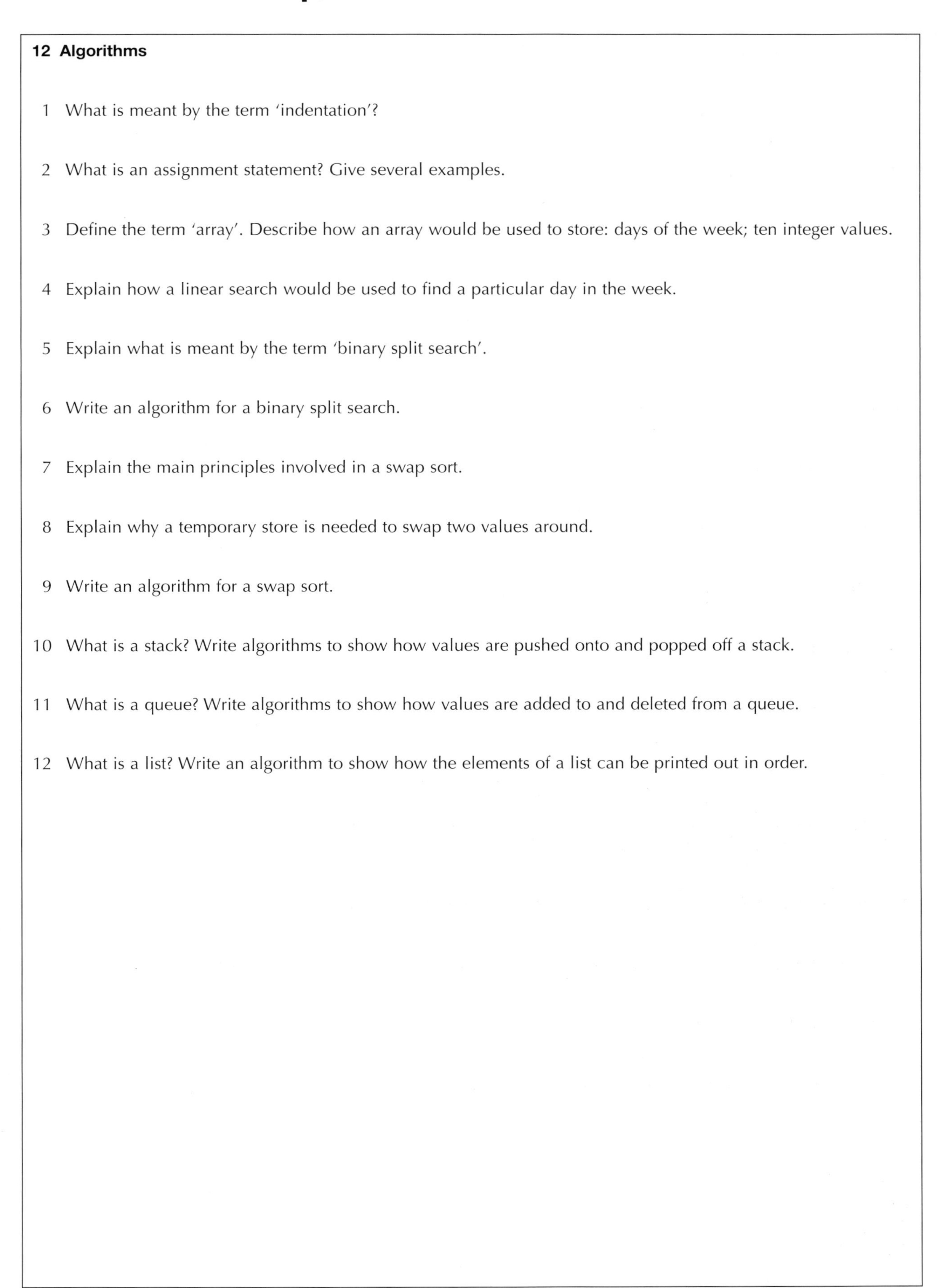

12 Algorithms

1 What is meant by the term 'indentation'?

2 What is an assignment statement? Give several examples.

3 Define the term 'array'. Describe how an array would be used to store: days of the week; ten integer values.

4 Explain how a linear search would be used to find a particular day in the week.

5 Explain what is meant by the term 'binary split search'.

6 Write an algorithm for a binary split search.

7 Explain the main principles involved in a swap sort.

8 Explain why a temporary store is needed to swap two values around.

9 Write an algorithm for a swap sort.

10 What is a stack? Write algorithms to show how values are pushed onto and popped off a stack.

11 What is a queue? Write algorithms to show how values are added to and deleted from a queue.

12 What is a list? Write an algorithm to show how the elements of a list can be printed out in order.

Index